GOD IN WORK

'A brave and prophetic book' – *Third Way*

'Important' – *Church Times*

Christian Schumacher is the son of refugees from Hitler's Germany – his father went on to write the classic book *Small is Beautiful*. Christian studied politics, philosophy and economics at Oxford before joining the steel industry as a management trainee and subsequently became an organizational consultant for British Steel, advising on the restructuring of steel plants. He held a fellowship at the London School of Economics for two years before establishing his own consultancy. He has been involved in the successful reorganization of a wide variety of British and overseas companies and public-sector organizations. He and his wife Diana live in Surrey. They have two grown-up daughters.

GOD IN WORK

CHRISTIAN SCHUMACHER

A LION BOOK

Published by
Lion Publishing plc
Sandy Lane West, Oxford, England
www.lion-publishing.co.uk
ISBN 0 7459 4043 9

Hardback edition 1998
Paperback edition 1999
10 9 8 7 6 5 4 3 2 1 0

Acknowledgments
Scripture extracts are reproduced from the New Revised
Standard Version of the Bible, copyright © 1989 by the
Division of Christian Education of the National Council
of the Churches of Christ in the USA, and the HOLY BIBLE,
NEW INTERNATIONAL VERSION. Copyright © 1973,
1978, 1984 by the International Bible Society. Hodder and
Stoughton Ltd. All rights reserved.

A catalogue record for this book is available
from the British Library

Printed and bound in Great Britain by
Caledonian International Book Manufacturing, Glasgow

Contents

Introduction

Very many people, young and old, are deeply fearful for the future of our civilization on Planet Earth. There is a growing awareness that the huge forces that are driving modern industrial society onwards are becoming dangerously out of control. Massive and interrelated problems are arising which nobody knows how to solve. Global warming; the melting of the polar ice caps; the hole in the ozone layer; growing environmental pollution of land, sea and air; the accelerating depletion of forests; the disappearance of countless animal and vegetable species; the worldwide decline in soil fertility; the uncontrollable sprawl of mega-cities and slums; the imminent exhaustion of many non-renewable raw materials, such as oil; the unchecked spiral of drugs, crime, disease and terrible poverty causing misery for millions in most countries of the world; the ruthless and reckless exploitation of international money markets; the armaments trade; wars; earthquakes; freak weather conditions – these are some of the current manifestations.

Christ prophesied the signs which will herald the end of the age:

You will hear of wars and rumours of wars, but see to it that you are not alarmed. Such things must happen, but the end is still to come. Nation will rise against nation, and kingdom against kingdom. There will be famines and earthquakes in various places. All these are the beginning of birth-pains.

Matthew 24:6–8 (NIV)

One is sometimes led to wonder: is the apocalypse near?

Since I was a child, I have been driven by a mounting desire to understand better the causes of these 'birth-pains'. Why is the world in such a mess, and how do we get out of it? We have all witnessed in our own lifetimes the pathological signs which are now threatening the very future of the planet itself. The global nature of the problem is uniquely one for our generation. I felt it particularly strongly, having been born into a refugee German family who fled from Hitler to England before World War II, and tasted personally some of the consequences of war and poverty. My parents' own concern for our future and for the environment also influenced me greatly.

Central to my search for some answers have been two axiomatic assumptions. The first is that there can be no solution to the problems of our times outside a religious perspective. I believe in God and have never had any doubt that as God created the universe and everything inside it, his imprint must be everywhere. Moreover, if God is pure goodness it is inconceivable that he would allow the present sufferings of the world to continue unabated without good reason and without giving mankind an infallible, all-powerful and practical remedy.

The remedy, therefore, lies with God. But how is this

remedy to be found, understood and applied by mankind? That is the real question. We know that our starting-point must be to grow closer to God. How is this to be done? Obviously, through the ways and means that God has given to the world's populations. What are these? Traditionally the way has always been associated with allegiance to an authentic religious tradition, in both East and West.

My way has been through the Christian tradition. I was brought up as a Christian, thanks mainly to my mother, and I have remained one, possibly because Christianity has dominated the part of the world in which I have lived. Christianity has also flourished in the places where the destructive forces largely responsible for the current global crises have been located. However, I do believe – and I hope that this book will show – that Christianity is in no way the cause of our modern predicaments. On the contrary, I am convinced that it holds the key to resolving (or at least understanding the root causes of) the world's problems. The question to be answered is: how can faith in God (and for Christians, belief in Jesus Christ and the Holy Spirit) help to overcome our current global crises? This is the quest of this book.

The second assumption governing the approach taken in this book is that, whatever may be the spiritual roots of our current predicament, nearly all the problems we currently encounter have stemmed from the way nature has been ruthlessly exploited to meet our material desires. In other words, the secular causes of our modern predicament are to be found in the phenomenon of industrial work and more generally in the way science and technology have been used to fashion it. Industrial work has been the defining feature of modern civilization. Indeed, so dominant has it been that we actually call ourselves an 'industrial society' in recognition of the unique contribution industrial work has made to our lives – in sharp contrast to previous forms of civilization: agrarian, feudal, nomadic, and so forth.

This book explores the nature of industrial work from both a Christian and a scientific point of view. It will attempt to show how our understanding of God can offer profound insights into how the reorganization of human work can contribute towards making our society 'whole'. I will argue that there are practical and achievable patterns of work which conform to God's will for us and that it is possible and, indeed, essential that industrial work is made to conform to these patterns in order to solve our global problems. The thesis will be supported by social science evidence. The book will also examine the relation between 'whole' or holy work and 'deformed' work; and between work and the wider society which it has shaped. It will argue that work has become deformed because it no longer conforms to the pattern set by God, and that this is one of the main roots of our global problems.

The book will also argue that, conversely, 'whole' work can lead to a 'whole' society and, with God's help, the runaway global crises now afflicting us can be reduced, if not averted altogether. What is more, we personally can do something about it. It is actually possible for each of us, in a myriad of small ways, to help save the planet. Perhaps we may even be contributing towards the fulfilment of Christ's promise of 'a new heaven and a new earth'.

The format of the book is chronological and autobiographical. It tells the story of my own search for meaning in relation to the world of work; how it began, evolved and matured to the point where theological insight and empirical observation became mutually reinforcing.

The ideas expressed in this book are based on practice as much as theory. I spent sixteen years of my working life in the iron and steel industry and another twenty years as a practising management consultant. I have worked in production, commercial and strategic functions. As a consultant I have advised some of the world's largest companies, as well as healthcare organizations, educational establishments and central and local governments. I have worked in Great Britain, continental Europe and overseas. I mention these facts in the hope that recounting my own experiences will encourage others. To add some colour to the narrative a number of case studies are also described in which industrial work has been designed on the basis of Christian principles with exciting benefits to people and planet alike.

The book is intended mainly for anyone who is acquainted with the world of industrial work, who is unhappy with it, who has been brought up, nominally at least, in the Christian tradition, and who is looking for an authentic Christian contribution to redeeming work. An expert knowledge of scripture and of the historically accepted doctrines of the mainstream Christian churches is not required by the reader.

To whet the appetite, or perhaps arouse the reader's curiosity, let me say that the remedy for the redemption of industrial work is not to be found explicitly in the biblical texts since the Bible only describes work in conditions prevailing in the largely rural and nomadic Middle Eastern world of two thousand and more years ago. The exciting discovery developed in this book is that the link between scripture and industrial work is to be found in the profound extrapolations from scripture which can be found in Christian theology.

Unfortunately, the word 'theology' today has a bad name. It tends to be used disparagingly. When arguments become obscurely theoretical or bigoted they are dismissed as 'theological'. The implication is that theology is not worth studying. In fact nothing could be further from the truth. Until recently, theology used to be called 'the queen of the sciences' and this book will seek to show it still is. Moreover, it will show that the main theological insights acquired over the past two millennia are crucial to understanding and solving the problems of modern industrial work.

This is not to say that contemporary Christianity has up to now had little to say about the world of work. The churches have intervened in four main areas. First, and most dominant, has been an emphasis on personal witness and behaviour. The Christian is exhorted to 'love one's neighbour' at work, to pray and to practise the virtues as exemplified in the Beatitudes and elsewhere in scripture. Second, the churches have made a strong contribution to the field of business ethics. Christian businessmen and -women are urged to treat their employees fairly, to invest in ethically sound ventures, to support ethical boardroom policies and so on. Third, there is a growing body of Christian thought about right leadership, usually modelled on the example of Christ himself, as servant. And fourth, there is an impressive body of social teaching which focuses on the inalienable rights of the worker, rights to employment, to humane working conditions, freedom to join a trade union, etc.

The trouble is that none of these areas of intervention have so far been capable of overcoming the major global crises of the modern era. The unpalatable truth is that despite its positive contributions, Christianity is still increasingly finding itself at the margins of industrial, let alone global, decision-making. Indeed, there is a clamour of voices claiming that religion should have nothing to do with secular matters at all but should stick to the spiritual task of saving souls, and leave economics to the economists, politics to the politicians and industry to the industrialists.

The fact that contemporary Christianity appears to be making little impact does not mean that there is no impact to be made. This book will argue that within theology there is, indeed, an authentic Christian response which is biblically sound, is compatible with the teachings of the church, is directly accessible to all Christians and non-Christians alike, and is so powerful and compelling that it can make a decisive difference to our global future.

I hope that the reader will consider carefully the arguments put forward and not dismiss theology out of hand. This book will attempt to show that theology can give a clarity and depth of insight which is awesome in its power. The Christian churches have in their possession an immense treasury of wisdom contained in the credal theology of the great Fathers of the church and their successors. This book will seek to show how apt are their insights and how relevant they are to understanding the real nature of industrial work and its relation to the global crises. Contrast this with the often dismal contributions of the secular sciences, which are often contradictory, excessively complex and usually superficial! In any case, modern science alone cannot solve the problems it itself has created. Indeed, the global crises testify that modern science and technology are condemned by their own actions. By contrast, the theologically grounded vision explored in this book offers an exciting, realistic, people-centred and sustainable hope for the future.

I have tried to keep the book practical and accessible to the reader. The ideas are intended to be used by the average lay person. The book will explain how to identify the pattern set by God for our own work, and how we can bring it about in our own surroundings. The theological and social science jargon has also been kept to a minimum.

In preparing this book I have enjoyed the support and encouragement of a large number of people from all walks of life and religious and secular persuasions. I want to say a big 'thank you' to them all, and especially to Diana, my wife, and also to my wider family for their tolerance and perseverance.

I also hope that the reader will be as excited and stimulated by the subject matter as I have been. I take heart from a letter sent to me by a young student who, after reading the manuscript, wrote:

I had often felt as a Christian in the working environment there was a limit to one's witness, and I did not know how God could be found in the structure of work. I had also often wondered how one could ever reach one's true potential as a Christian at work and why on earth did God seem to lead people (most people) into the everyday drudgery of 'routine' work? Your writings certainly open up a whole new dimension of thinking which I believe could be presented to Christians at all levels of intelligence and status, assisting them to bring God more into work and explaining how they can see him actively working there already! I also think your book could be a marvellous witness to a businessman/company, presenting them with the principles and then implementing them for all to see the transformation!

This book is an offering to all those who are also searching for meaning within industrial work as we experience the dark, unintelligible and frightening birth-pains of our age.

CHAPTER 1

Spiritual Awakenings

I don't remember much about my early childhood, perhaps because it was painful. I was born in London in 1937, and with World War II looming my parents became political refugees from Hitler's Germany. We lived in a small primitive cottage in a wood, outside the village of Eydon in Northamptonshire. For many years I mistakenly thought it was spelt 'Eden'. I am glad it wasn't. We suffered poverty and some persecution in the bitter years of the war. My father earned two pounds per week as a farm labourer, and supported my mother, myself and my new younger brother John, together with two homeless refugees who used to bath me in an aluminium tub on the kitchen table with cold water.

We lived in constant fear of reprisals from the nearby villagers who, not unnaturally, suspected and disliked the Germans. Once a gang of village men came to the cottage with sticks, to threaten to drive our family away. No one played with us. I was lonely as a child. But I loved the woods and the fields, the secret life of the forest and the farm. My earliest memories were of the mixture of curiosity and fear, as we were chased by a bull while walking in a farmer's field; of climbing trees until I could go no higher; of helping my father chop wood; and of being naughty.

Perhaps it was the woods that first evoked that sense of mystery, awe and peace which later turned into a belief in God. Or maybe it was the contrast between that peace and the enveloping war, between the rustle of leaves and the mechanical drone of the V-2 bombs. I don't know. But I remember the bitter-sweet feeling of estrangement from the violent, incomprehensible world of men, and the warmth of my own private world in the woods.

By the time I was fourteen years old we had moved house seven times: Weybridge, Eydon, Oxford, London, Berlin, Frankfurt and Caterham in Surrey. Immediately after the war in 1946 my father was sent to Berlin with the British government. When we arrived in the icy winter of 1946–47 the city was devastated: rubble, people living in cellars, in makeshift shacks or huddled in the bombed-out ruins of the remaining upright buildings. The city was divided into British, French, American and Russian sectors. We lived in a requisitioned house on the edge of a city park, called the Grunewald. My brother John and I spent many hours exploring the 'Green Wood'. In the grim aftermath of war, it was littered with the debris of destruction; with unexploded shells, broken vehicles and tanks, twisted metal and torn-down trees. I remember a derelict bombed-out cellar in which lived a pack of abandoned Alsatian dogs. I remember walking through the grey broken streets, past soldiers and the cowed silence of the penniless city dwellers, for whom a cigarette was their only means of exchange.

It was in Berlin where I first met the devil; not literally, thankfully, but in the imagination. One of my brother John's and my greatest joys was an old army torch which we had been given, and which had red, blue, green and yellow light filters. At night in bed we used to play the 'devil game'. We imagined that we lived in a huge skyscraper. The devil could supply us with any luxury we could desire. All we needed to do was to ask, and we asked and asked. We took it in turns to play the devil by shining the torch on our own faces, illuminating them in grotesque colours.

No doubt there are psychological explanations for our game, which stemmed from the horrors of war. But why, I have wondered many times, did we as young children invoke the devil? I don't know, but as I look back on my life, I can see that the battle between good and evil, right and wrong, austerity and wealth, has been a constant theme. I see also that my belief in the supremacy of good has far outweighed the evils we were then experiencing. This feeling was reinforced when our family returned to England in 1950, I having been despatched to a boarding prep school in Hampshire.

It was a kind school, admirably run by a Mr Whitehouse and his sister. There, despite the bullying of 'that German boy', I began to discover a modest prowess in sport and music. I especially loved being in the choir, and looked forward to the weekly one-mile walks to the nearby village of West Meon, where the school attended morning worship on Sundays. I was joint head chorister with my friend

19

Michael Sandell, and we were both allowed to sing descant in our clear treble voices. At that time I had quite unrealistic pretensions of being a composer. I fancied I could hear Beethovenesque symphonies cascading through my inner ear – if only I knew how to write them down! In the event, our long-suffering music teacher transcribed the musical score of the only song I ever composed (which I was convinced would be a bestseller) and sent it to the BBC. The text was:

Life is only a dream
However queer it may seem
However queer it may seem
Life is only a dream.

By that age I was amply used to rejection, so when the BBC returned the score with the recommendation that I should try 'Children's Hour', not many tears were shed.

But this musical awakening aroused another part of my soul – I discovered the magic of the church organ and the liturgy. Within the quiet serenity of the church in West Meon, reinforced by the regularity of our visits, I began to experience a silent, inner peace, a tiny oasis which left the struggle for survival far behind.

It wasn't the first time that a foretaste of paradise beckoned. My parents had never given up the German way of celebrating Christmas. It started with the first Sunday of Advent, which was marked by a single candle, lighted at teatime. Each day we were allowed to open a tiny present, a piece of chocolate, a biscuit, or once, I remember, a thimble beautifully wrapped and hanging on a coloured string. On the second Sunday, there would be two candles, on the third, three. On Christmas Eve the door of our living-room was locked and the curtains drawn. We had to dress in our best clothes for the Christmas celebration, which began in the early evening. Our family and some friends (who were always invited) assembled outside the door. Excitement mounted. My mother led us in singing some Christmas carols, always ending with the beautiful 'Silent Night'. At the last chord, my father, who was in the Christmas room, would ring a silver bell, and the door would be opened. One by one, the youngest first, we would be allowed in the room – and a glimpse of heaven. The room was bathed in the soft yellow light of flickering candles, and colourful Christmas decorations. At the end stood the Christmas tree, majestic from floor to ceiling, silver tinsel shining in the light of more candles, like sentries on the trees' branches; interspersed with little wooden angels, stars, gingerbread, sweets and gold and silver bulbs. In front, made of rough stone, the family of Jesus crowded around the manger, with the cattle and the shepherds, the wise men and their gifts.

I cannot describe the joy which we as children felt at that sight, despite the fact that – I have to confess – our aesthetic and religious sensibilities were somewhat dulled by the shadowy sight of the Christmas presents concealed behind the tree! But 'grab and run' was strictly forbidden. God had to be thanked before presents could be opened. My parents followed a traditional course, practised for many generations. Before the presents came the Christmas service. This consisted of readings, carol singing and, not least, contributions by the children of music and poetry which we had practised especially for the occasion.

So it was that as a small boy the seeds of faith were born in me.

Of course I did not understand anything with my mind. I didn't need to, because little by little God was entering my soul through the beauty of his creation. I also failed to perceive the influence of my mother's own deep faith. She was the epitome of love: spontaneous, ever-patient, consistently kind, long-suffering and with a deep Christian faith which never doubted for a second. Right up to her death of cancer – she was only forty-nine years old when she died – she was the bond holding the family together. She loved to the end and God rewarded her. Her last words, as her life drained away, were 'I am so happy, so happy.'

My school years were a process of catching up. The war had dislocated our education, and as refugees constantly on the move my brother and I had little inclination or opportunity to worry about the three Rs. So when serious schooling began, it was always a struggle: my position in class was usually twenty-ninth out of thirty-two! However, the lack of academic success was amply compensated for by a certain ability in most sports, especially hockey and rugby. This endeared me more to Mr McIntyre, the PE teacher, than to the headmaster, whose periodic 'chats' with my parents, and their subsequent remonstrations with me, made little impact. Throughout my life, up to then, I had been more concerned with keeping out of trouble than with academic achievement, and this was more a question of outwitting the teachers than memorizing dreary syntax. I wasn't against lessons, but they failed to motivate me. Chemistry was a good example. I remember once asking the teacher why it was that hydrogen and oxygen combined to make water. The answer was typical of the autocratic teaching methods of the time, 'Never mind why, just accept that they do.' But that was impossible for an inquisitive mind, and the thought that I would have to memorize many other formulae without understanding any of them, put me off chemistry for the rest of my student days.

Gradually I caught up academically. Having made very hard work of O levels (GCSEs), I found A levels less arduous. I had no idea what I wanted to do in life, so I thought to keep options open by studying two arts subjects (History and Latin) and two science subjects (Pure Maths and Applied Maths). By this time, too, I was beginning to search more consciously for some pattern of meaning to life, and was starting to question conventional wisdom and values. My father was an enormous influence. Temperamentally he was the antithesis of my mother. She was warm, loving, emotional, caring, devout; he was the radical intellectual with a ceaselessly active enquiring mind, caught up in Nietzsche, Schopenhauer, and the idealism of the Utopian socialists of the 1930s.

As my sister, Barbara, has written in *Alias Papa* (the biography of our father), after his return to England in 1950 his own intellectual journey had taken him beyond the nihilism of the German philosophers and its social expression in Marxism and radical socialism. He was seeking a deeper truth which led him, during the 1950s, to discover the great spiritual traditions of the East, in particular Buddhism. Thanks in part to a very unusual bookshop in Cecil Court, London, (called Stuart and Watkins in those days) my father had acquired a formidable library of philosophical, religious, mystical, esoteric and spiritual books from many traditions. These ranged from the great religions such as Buddhism, Hinduism and Islam, to a series of more recent sages (and I suspect some charlatans) from Gurdjieff and Ouspensky, Rudolf Steiner, Gandhi, the Maharishi and J. G. Bennett to Adams and *Flying Saucers Have Landed*.

As a teenager I was fascinated by this cornucopia of wisdom, by the sheer breadth and volume of writings on the supernatural, on mysticism and mystery, on sages and Sufism. I would browse for hours in my father's study, sampling the new books coming in, revisiting the old. My father willingly encouraged these researches, discreetly prodding me to investigate this book or that. He rarely expressed his own views about religious or spiritual matters, however, even when questioned. On the other hand, he would talk for hours about his economic ideas, whether on the coal industry (where he was economic adviser at the National Coal Board) or on his fast-growing interest in the economics of developing countries. In 1952 he had been invited to Burma on contract for three months. During his stay, and stimulated by his growing fascination with Eastern religions, he used to spend his weekends at a Buddhist monastery. He returned to England with the concept of 'intermediate technology' which he described in a paper which was the forerunner of the chapter in his book *Small is Beautiful* entitled 'Buddhist economics'. His seminal insight had been to apply the Buddhist precepts of non-violence, respect for nature and the 'middle way' to technology.

As an ordinary schoolboy, I had no inkling of the revolutionary importance of my father's ideas, nor of the enormous influence they were having on my own thinking. Indeed it was only in 1960, with the publication of an article on intermediate technology in the *Observer* newspaper, that my father began to receive public recognition. At home we took his thinking completely for granted, untarnished by the economic orthodoxy of the day.

In terms of religious or spiritual matters, however, it was a different story. I was left to find my own way. Why my father did not share his developing faith with the family was a mystery. Was he perhaps not sure enough of his own beliefs? Or maybe he knew that his children would have to find their own way? Or did he leave our religious upbringing to our devout and loving mother? In any event, by the age of seventeen, my views on religion were muddled to say the least. I remember believing that this world was an illusion, that mankind was 'asleep', and that somewhere, somehow, there existed another, better realm. I was also very keen to find it! But how? I believed that the solution lay in raising one's own level of consciousness; in accomplishing a better control of one's mind; in meditation and self-denial. Vainly I sought to accomplish this!

However, by the age of nineteen I was becoming even

more confused. I was no longer sure that meditation and self-control were the answer. They were arid experiences, and anyway I wasn't very good at them. Worse, they seemed to confirm my egocentricity. In trying to keep out of my mind images of the world outside, I simply filled it with an inflated awareness of myself. Also I had no idea how all this connected with the gospel of Jesus Christ, in whose power I was increasingly being drawn to believe.

CHAPTER 2

Framing some Questions

Having left school with a sigh of relief in December 1956, I was called up to do National Service in February 1957. Fortune smiled and, mainly due to my hockey prowess, I was commissioned in the Royal Engineers and spent my time playing hockey and making maps in Cyprus. Apart from being a beautiful island, Cyprus was a formative experience in many ways. It was the time of the EOKA terrorism. I had command of a platoon but possessed few leadership skills; and we were under canvas for a year in emergency conditions. Yet I enjoyed the experience thoroughly, and was glad of the opportunity to serve the country. National Service was an adventurous, confidence-building experience, and one which incidentally I would strongly recommend for young people today.

In the army I grew up. The army taught one discipline, self-responsibility, loyalty and the art of living closely with others in difficult circumstances. I was demobbed in 1959, thoroughly physically fit, optimistic about the future and, most importantly, with my values and beliefs undamaged. Indeed, from the rigours of the soldier's life, they emerged enriched through the experiences of other peoples, other cultures and other places.

After spending six months exploring Canada and the USA, I went to New College, Oxford, to read Politics, Philosophy and Economics. In contrast to my father, who had also briefly attended New College as a Rhodes scholar, these were by far the happiest, most productive and most privileged years of my life thus far.

I was intoxicated by the many delights of the place: the dreaming spires, college gardens, scouts, the Bodleian, tutorials, cricket, punts, church bells, gowns, digs, proctors, and secret routes into college after midnight (there were even false bars on my own window in the New College quadrangle). Like so many generations before and since, I was enchanted by its sheer munificence – where every interest could be pursued and every human faculty developed, whether spiritual, intellectual or physical. With the compulsive enthusiasm of the typical student I plunged into activities of every kind. As time was short it had to be organized, so consequently the days were spent in a mixture of five pursuits: academic work, sport, social life, hobbies and good causes (but not in that order of importance!). It was at Oxford that I learned the truth of the old saying 'Education is what you have left after you have forgotten everything you have ever learned.'

Top of the list of my priorities during my last year was a beautiful, dark-haired and slender undergraduate reading history at St Hilda's. Judging by the number of other admirers and suitors surrounding her, and the number of parties and dances to which she was consistently invited, the frequently heard comparisons with Zuleika Dobson were not inappropriate. Diana Binns, for that was her name, was born in Burma, the daughter of a plantation manager. We met by chance at a War on Want lunch, where she was accompanied by a friend, and where she dazzled everyone with her lovely smile, charm and intelligent wit. As organizer of the event, I tried to make use of my slight tactical advantage and asked nervously if I could see her again. There did not seem much space in her social diary before the end of term, but I managed to persuade her to come out to dinner, which became the first of many romantic encounters and adventures. We eventually married just after two years later, when she had left Oxford and I had completed the first year of my first job.

Oxford also taught me how to think! It was there that those intellectual stirrings which had been slowly emerging throughout my life came to the surface. The combination of politics, philosophy and economics gave a panoramic overview of the secular forces shaping our civilization, especially since I was taught by such stimulating teachers as Roger Opie, Harry Nicholas, Isaiah Berlin and Anthony Quinton. Not that I agreed with everything they said, nor did I like much of what I learned. In particular, I was bitterly disappointed with the obscure triviality and irrelevance of the so-called Oxford School of Philosophy. Not only did it not provide answers to any of the critical existential and moral issues of the day – the nature of man and his destiny on the planet – but it did not even ask the questions. The possibility of the existence of God wasn't mentioned once. Politics was nearly as bad. What we learned about was some political history, a dismal collection of outdated political theories and a long list of parliamentary rituals. Hardly ever did we glimpse a nobleness of purpose, a dedication to the public good, and a statesmanlike vision for the future well-being of our culture and society.

I enjoyed economics most, partly due to the teaching skills of Roger Opie (he treated me as a friend) and partly because I could draw on the refreshing sustenance of my father's ideas. Also, as my father had worked at Oxford during the early years of the war, he had a number of close acquaintances who had since become eminent economics dons, such as Professors Balogh and Worswick, at whose feet I sat. We were allocated two 'special' subjects and I specialized in the economics of developing countries and, by contrast, in monetary economics.

Despite the apparent irrelevance (in my opinion at the time) of much of the academic syllabus to 'real life', the reality was that I was becoming more and more aware of some of the really big questions facing contemporary society. What was it that made the economic system condemn two-thirds of the world to live in poverty, while a small number of multi-millionaires could manipulate the money market with impunity? How could political systems suck the world into the icy grip of the Cold War with the Russians, who seemed to me to be quite sympathetic as a people? Why did regimes as vicious as the communists under Stalin and Kruschev exist and survive for so long? And – a question that increasingly fascinated me – what were the fundamental forces driving our modern Western industrial society, and where were they leading us?

Oxford was an ideal place to debate these and many similar questions, if not in formal sessions then informally amongst friends, late at night over coffee. In this atmosphere opinions were formed and lifelong friends were made: people of widely different values and beliefs, but sharing the exuberance of student life.

During those happy days, my Christian life took a new turn. I still loved singing hymns in church, the beauty of the liturgy and the deep resonances of the 1662 Prayer Book. To this day I am deeply moved by the priest solemnly presiding at the Eucharist, performing the sacrifice of the Mass by word and gesture, arms outstretched, head bowed. In New College Chapel I experienced everything the Church of England did best. The setting was magnificent: the ancient carved oak pews; the intricately ornamental reredos; the despairing, twisted stone sculpture of Lazarus by Epstein; the vaulted ceilings and rich stained-glass windows. And above all I loved the New College choir, world famous for the clear pure beauty of its boy trebles and the scholarly perfection of the counter-tenors, baritones and basses.

Within these religious emotions, however, something else was stirring in my soul. I was being made increasingly aware that on its own, the serenity of the church service was beginning to taste of self-indulgence, almost an escape from the world. Not that this was wrong in itself. My religious experiences were real and vivid. I felt God was really present in the Eucharist and in the liturgy, and I loved the beauty of his presence.

Yet on its own, to worship wasn't enough. The God of the universe was not allowing me to rest complacently in his temple, while outside the world was racked with war, disease, poverty and injustice. New thoughts began persistently to gnaw at my conscience. Why was the world outside in such disarray? What could I do to make things better? And what help could I expect from God? My mind was beginning to demand an explanation of the relevance of Christianity to the major issues of the day. In particular I wanted to know why, if God created the world, it was in such a mess. More importantly, did it have to be in such a mess?

Gradually these thoughts took hold and emerged as a single line of reasoning, culminating in a question. God was the creator of the world, and God was supremely good. Manifestly the world wasn't good. Mankind, and not God, had obviously therefore spoilt it. But if God was good, a solution to the mess must ostensibly exist, not only intellectually and theoretically, but in a way which people could actually put into practice. So what was it? Where in Christianity did the answer lie? After all, Christ himself had said 'I am the Way, the Truth and the Life.' The trouble was that nothing that I then associated with Christianity convincingly pointed to a 'blueprint for survival'. Yes, my private world of faith and worship meant a lot, but it didn't embrace the whole domain of human concern. What, I increasingly asked myself, did Christmas, Easter, Whitsun, baptisms, marriages, funerals, the chalice, hymns, vestments, churches and Sundays have to do with relieving poverty, stopping wars, helping the sick and reversing the tide of materialism and selfishness which was eating at the heart of our social and economic life, and pushing society towards self-destruction? Christianity, as I understood it, appeared largely irrelevant in addressing these questions, let alone those posed by the physical sciences, engineering, politics, social affairs, psychology, anthropology and the rest of the disciplines. Religion seemed to exist in a world of its own, confined to Sundays and certain listed buildings. Even the undergraduates who at Oxford were associated with the numerous Christian societies often gave the impression of being isolated and inward-looking, sometimes drab, often judgmental and narrow-minded. One couldn't easily go to the pub or laugh at a joke with many of them.

So what had gone wrong? Why wasn't Christianity holding centre stage? After all, if God created the world, not even one single speck of dust could exist for a fraction of a second without him, let alone the whole of nature – earth, air, fire and water – or the whole of the human domain – science, technology, politics, philosophy, economics and the rest. I felt that with God's omnipotence there had to exist somewhere a divine plan for the world, which could heal the confusion and tragedies afflicting mankind. But what was it? Where could it be found? I began to be convinced that whole areas of Christianity, possibly its central features, were being neglected by the churches – perhaps they had been forgotten – and that if one could discover them, one would hold the key to understanding the world's predicaments and how to transcend them. Then God would again hold his rightful place as Lord of all creation, not by imposing a miserable Cromwellian puritanism on everyone, but in glorious splendour and good humour, lifting the heart, bringing out the best in intellectual achievement, aesthetic accomplishment, intense personal happiness and love for one another. I was determined to find the key.

When Oxford came to an end, although I loved every minute of it, I was not sorry to leave. I not only wanted to get into 'real life', to earn a living in my own right, but more importantly, I was full of youthful zeal to find out at first hand what made our Western industrial society tick. After all, we were an industrial society, something no other civilization had been. Industrial work was the distinguishing feature. There had been agricultural societies before, nomadic tribes, societies based on serfdom, feudalism, conquest and hunting, but never on the systematic application of science and technology – on industrial work. To understand work and its relation to God was surely the key to understanding God's plan for the modern world.

Work was the clue. I was convinced that the aberrations to be found in our way of life were connected with a degree of estrangement from God that had something to do with the way we lived and worked. Somehow industrial society had divorced itself from God, and I intended to find out why and how. God's natural creation – the woods, flowers, trees and the sweet sounds of the birds – was being denied to most people. How could young couples like us, for example, living in a soulless maisonette in Ealing, West London, be sensitive to God through the rhythm of the day and the night, through the subtle songs of the countryside, through the never-ceasing cycle of spring, summer, autumn and winter – when their only outdoor experience was the journey to the supermarket or the station to catch the 8.15 a.m. commuter train to central London? Did people's estrangement from God stem perhaps from the artificial nature of their working lives? From the complex urban/industrial structures in which they lived and worked? I was determined to find out more about the essential nature of these industrial structures.

One way to begin, I thought, was to go into industry. I therefore found a job in a steel company, and started with Stewarts & Lloyds Ltd in September 1962. I must confess to not having been in the slightest degree interested in their products, steel tubes. I joined because the blast furnace was held to be the womb of the industrial revolution, and I wanted to experience working there at first hand. If there was to be an answer to our industrial predicament, the steel industry was likely to be as good a place as any to look for major clues. So, full of hope and self-confidence (there is no one more arrogant than a new graduate entering his first job), I began my new life.

I was very quickly brought down to earth with an unpleasant thud. My first job was as a trainee in a sales office in Glasgow. There were about thirty people in the office and our job was to receive enquiries and orders for steel from customers. We had to transcribe the documentation onto the firm's paperwork, fill in all the customers' details, and then pass the information to the factories where the steel was made. I remember the office well: the thirty people, each at a separate desk, were spaced out in rows, a lot of hard work to do, very routine work, basically filling in the same forms all day long, and passing them on to somebody else. We used to do this for seven to eight hours a day, five days a week, week after week. I only did it for three months, but there were some people who had been there for twenty years doing exactly the same work. They were in a terrible rut. They used to go home in the evening and the next day would come back and the whole cycle was repeated.

I would often ask myself 'What does Christianity have to do with all this? What is the connection between one's belief in God and one's regular visits to church on Sundays, with its hymns and liturgy and prayers, and the meaningless drudgery of one's working life?' I had great difficulty reconciling the two worlds. At best I could see that my place of work was an arena in which one could possibly 'love one's neighbour'. I could give a cheery smile to the lady who brought round the tea trolley, perhaps, or listen to somebody who had a problem at home – but that was about the extent of it. Otherwise there was little opportunity to exercise my religious faith in that environment. One problem was that the desks were spaced so far apart that one couldn't talk to other people, even if one wanted to. Also, we were busy and social chit-chat was in any case discouraged. So what does it mean to 'love one's neighbour' in an environment like that? I couldn't see it. It was very discouraging.

Next I was sent to a steelworks in Corby, Northamptonshire, where I worked inside the factory itself. I remember taking Diana to see the site, and she was so appalled by the smoke, fire and hissing steam of those 'dark Satanic mills' that she burst into tears! In the mill in which I worked there were about 200 people, most of them process workers, and many had been there for many years. The work was dangerous, monotonous, physically demanding and unforgiving. I suspected also that some of the steel produced was going into armaments and other uses which, with a clear conscience, I couldn't square with the Gospels. Nor could I see what more a belief in Christianity could do to improve such a place, compared with a mere secular humanism. If God created the universe it ought to be blindingly obvious what a Christian agenda should be, but it wasn't. Later the steelworks was shut down and the workforce went on the dole. I asked myself, 'What happens now to the men without any work at all? What does the Christian church have to offer these people?' There were lots of unanswered questions.

Diana and I were married at that time, and we moved down to London where I got a job with an economic consultancy, Maxwell Stamp Associates. Having failed to find any convincing connections between Christianity and the micro-world of clerical and industrial work, perhaps there were some ties with the wider economic realms. I enjoyed consultancy work very much, and was involved in a variety of tasks from writing half-yearly 'country reports' on the financial state of thirty-five countries, to advising a client whether or not to build a salt mine in Portugal, to presenting a business case for building a railway in Tanzania, to assessing the prospects for the UK cotton industry. While the work certainly helped to broaden my field of economic vision, and taught me how to find my way through a maze of statistics and economic indicators, it again did very little to unravel any of the more fundamental questions I was asking. What really was the relevance of Christianity to the forces driving the worldwide system of trade and business? Did economic development conform with God's plan for humanity, or did it not – and why? Were there divinely imposed criteria which must be met if the world was to survive and prosper, and if so – what? The present system was clearly exploitative and wasteful of resources, and I felt a growing unease that it was gradually spinning out of control. The mad rush for unlimited economic growth could not go on for ever. So why was the church so strangely silent? Again, I could find no answers.

Two years later I got a job in the Civil Service. As it happened, it was in the part of the Civil Service looking after the steel industry. This was before steel was nationalized in 1967. Although in a junior position, I found myself in the so-called 'corridors of power'. My first job was to look at pricing policy. The Iron & Steel Board was responsible for deciding what to charge for the steel. There were arguments about whether customers should be given a discount if they were long-standing, faithful and regular customers; or if they bought over a certain quantity of steel. We also had to do some cost analyses of applications to build new steelworks. We had to work out whether or not to give permission to go ahead on the basis of whether the market was big enough, whether the costs were competitive, and whether the applicants could made a profit. We worked very hard. I remember once that we had to prepare a paper on whether or not it was advantageous to join the Common Market. That was a pretty difficult question, even in economic terms. But what did Christianity have to say on issues like these? On investment and pricing decisions? I couldn't find any connections at all. Yet surely, I thought, these are very important questions for the future of our society. Surely, an all-powerful, all-loving God ought to have something of relevance to say. After all, it was the Christian religion which historically changed the entire face of the Western world after the days of the Roman empire. Surely it hadn't run out of steam today! I couldn't escape the profound conviction that there must be an intimate connection between love, Jesus, God the creator of the universe and the big economic and social questions of the day. But what this might be, I hadn't a clue.

After steel was nationalized in 1967, my career took me to rather different pastures. The Iron & Steel Board had become the 'chairman's office' of the newly formed British Steel Corporation. Lord Melchett was the first chairman, and I worked under his senior strategic adviser, Jim Driscoll. Later I moved to the personnel department. I thought perhaps here, in the people side of the business, I could find some clues as to what the connection was between one's Christian faith and one's work. After all, this was where the 'people issues' were being dealt with, such as industrial relations and trade-union issues, employee welfare, and so on. We were faced with questions such as 'How much should people be paid?' 'What should be their conditions of employment?'

In the event, from a Christian point of view, I was again disappointed with what I found. The personnel department seemed either to be concerned with administering rules and regulations, where the subject matter wasn't an order for steel, but was just a name or a number of a person; or else it seemed to be picking up the pieces after the human damage had occurred. A major industrial relations problem would arise in one of the steelworks, and the personnel department was then called in to sort it out. It was a little like a doctor being called in after the accident had happened. Again it didn't seem to me that God could be seen actively shaping his creation, even through those whose job it was to look after other people.

CHAPTER 3

The Way of Love

While I was at the Iron & Steel Board, and three years after Diana and I were married, we moved from our flat in Ealing, London, to a small cottage in Surrey. Many subsequent developments in our spiritual lives were directly linked to this move. Diana and I were not looking for a house in Surrey. We had met in Oxford: she was from Lincolnshire, I from Surrey. We had thought we would try to find a house somewhere of equal distance from each place. This 'textbook location' turned out to be in the middle of Heathrow Airport, so we had to start again. My father offered to let us build a house on some of his land, which Diana was to design with the help of an architect friend, but unfortunately it was in the Green Belt so the plan fell through. Then a friend of the family told us of a house in the same area which had just come on the market and we went to visit it. It was a charming Queen Anne cottage with climbing moss roses, inglenooks and alcoves, wooden panelling, small but perfectly proportioned and located opposite the village church.

As soon as we had stepped inside the front door, we

knew it was for us, not because of its charm alone, but because of the atmosphere. It was a 'happy house'. The owner began to show us round. After seeing just two rooms I looked at Diana, she nodded, and I offered the asking price, knowing that it was more than we could afford. 'Don't you want to look over the rest of the house first?' said the owner incredulously. Before I could answer the telephone rang and another prospective purchaser made an offer. He had been round on the previous day. I reminded the owner that we had made the first definite offer, and we secured the sale by five seconds! Later, unfortunately, we were gazumped but with a further act of faith offered and managed to match the new price. My grandfather's unexpected legacy came through just in time to secure the purchase.

We had many reasons for being thankful to God for the move, not least because there was a direct connection between our new home and the deepening of our spiritual lives. It happened quickly. Diana and I were in the habit of saying prayers and reading before we went to sleep at night. We were reading that lovely book *The Little Flowers of St Francis of Assisi*. It is a book that should be read aloud, if its inner spiritual beauty is to be really appreciated. St Francis had long been a favourite saint of ours, and it was a pleasure to read about his simple love of all God's creation, his humility and poverty, and the many amazing miracles and healings which accompanied him during his life.

It happened that we were invited to attend a religious meeting by some friends in the next village. We didn't quite know the purpose of the meeting, but Mel and Uvedale

Lambert were new friends, and we didn't want to let them down. There were about eight people present in a small upstairs room of a farmhouse. The speaker was a young Italian girl who spoke no English, and she was accompanied by a German girl who translated for her, but whose English was very little better. They falteringly told how, in 1943, a young woman from Trento in Italy had given her life to God and started a religious movement in Italy. As they spoke Diana and I became more and more incredulous. What we were hearing was a similar story to that of St Francis of Assisi, but one which was taking place in the twentieth century. The girls seemed to radiate the same simple joyous spirituality, the same intense love of God, the same gentle, deep and strong faith. They told of how a twenty-year-old teacher had been moved by God, had understood deeply that God is love and that she could be a mirror of God's love, by loving others unconditionally. They told how she attracted a small group of companions who survived the bombing of Trent during the war, and unstintingly helped the suffering people of the city. They explained how providence had helped them, and how many miracles occurred, how their numbers grew and their faith deepened. The movement was named the Focolare (the fire of the hearth). It spread rapidly and within twenty years some two million people worldwide were trying to live the same life of Christian love and service.

We were both deeply moved, not so much by what the Italian and German girls said, but by the simple, sincere and innocent way in which they said it. We could hardly believe our ears. What they were saying was that we didn't have to look back to the time of St Francis to find God intervening miraculously on earth. It was happening before our very eyes. There was living proof today of similar marvellous events taking place.

Diana was no longer working at this time and we decided at once to go to Italy to find out more for ourselves but we now had a three-month-old daughter, Christiana, whom Diana was feeding. Unfortunately, also, we had no money and could not afford the cost of the trip which amounted to some £160 for both of us. Nor did we wish to leave our daughter. Then, out of the blue, came a tax refund of £160 and Diana's mother offered to look after the baby saying that we both needed a holiday. So we set off thankfully for Rome.

From the moment we arrived at the Focolare Centre in Rocca di Papa near Rome, we realized that something very special was happening to us. The atmosphere was indescribably happy, the welcoming smiles unrestrained. During our five-day stay, we heard talks on the spirituality of the Focolare movement, visited Rome and the catacombs, had special seats at an audience with the Pope and, unforgettably, visited the Focolare village of Loppiano, near Florence, where 400 people live in a Christian community literally blazing with joy and love for one another.

Different people progress towards a spiritual understanding at different speeds and rhythms. Some start by struggling strenuously with doubt until slowly they emerge deeply strengthened; for others the route is smoother, punctuated evenly by insights and pitfalls; while others seem to need a period of severe suffering before their eyes are opened. For me, however, it was different again. I was simply overwhelmed. Instantaneously, with a blinding light, I experienced God as love. In the intensity of the joy I experienced at Rocca di Papa, my soul was shaken like a reed consumed by fire. It was as if I saw love face to face, the joy and suffering mixed, the agony and the ecstasy, crystal-clear understanding and fervent will combined. In youthful exuberance I resolved to throw myself wholeheartedly in the game of love.

Curiously, despite the profoundly moving encounters with the Focolare movement, I never seriously felt a calling to join them full time, though many others did: married couples, young boys and girls, including some friends of ours. I felt that my vocation lay elsewhere. While being asked to 'love my neighbour' like all Christians, I did not feel able to abandon my life utterly to the task – which Chiara Lubich, the founder of the Focolare movement, has called 'the work of Mary' – of bringing Christ to the world by following the rules of a particular religious movement. Those called to become Focolarini (in other words, full-time members of the Focolare movement) had given up their careers, left their homes to live in small communities, were sent to all parts of the world and took certain vows similar to those of other religious orders. This wasn't the route I wanted to follow.

Yet the trip was a turning-point in my inner life. Chiara and the Focolarini had spoken to my soul – and with a very simple formula. They simply loved, and by being channels of God, gave God to those they encountered. They gave the grace of being loved and also the strength to love others. Their aim was to create, through love, unity between all peoples, between rich and poor, black and white, friend and foe. They identified strongly with Jesus' last prayer 'that all of them may be one, Father, just as you are in me and I am in you'. It seemed fitting that out of the unity with nature, inspired by St Francis, God should lead me to understand the importance of unity between people, as espoused by Chiara Lubich. This insight was to have important implications later.

Of course, I had read about love many times before meeting the Focolare. The concept was nothing new. What was completely new to me was that the Focolarini practised loving quite literally, moment by moment. What is more, they loved me. They loved me without conditions, without a hidden agenda or an ulterior motive. I was accepted naturally and completely as their friend. Diana and I found ourselves among people – quite ordinary people from all walks of life – who were showing us by their actions and lifestyles that 'loving one another' wasn't a Utopian dream reserved only for a few saints. They were actually doing it, in both the little things and the big things of life. What was also new to me was that the Focolare possessed a methodology which, if followed, could increase one's own capacity to love. They showed us that to practise Christian love was an acquired skill. Diana and I could begin to learn without delay.

To practise Christian love, it is first necessary to know what is meant by it. Unfortunately the word 'love' has become so degraded and vulgarized, and so associated with sentimentality and self-gratification, that the very idea of 'loving one another' has become a cause of suspicion and scandal. The Focolarini therefore start by saying we should love other people as if they were Jesus himself, in other words, show them the same care, respect and consideration one would show to God if one were to meet him in the street. Now this is a tall order, so the Focolarini go on to stress that Christian love is basically a matter of the will, and not of the emotions. We have to go on loving even if we don't feel like it. This then enables the Christian to love everybody. We are asked to embrace all humanity without exception: black, white, rich, poor, our friends, those who don't interest us, and even those we positively dislike or who hate us. 'Love your enemies', said Jesus, 'and pray for them which despitefully use you or persecute you.' With human love, based as it is on our emotions, we are incapable of loving our enemies.

Second, the Focolarini teach that Christians should never put a limit on how much to love. They say that if we trust in Jesus' support, we can give everything to the other in love. We should therefore love without conditions; to the end. Human love, on the other hand, all too often peters out when the going gets too tough, or when the one who is loved does not respond in the way one expects. But Jesus said 'This is my commandment, that you love one another as I have loved you.' And he loved us to the point of dying for us. We too should be prepared to love our neighbour to the point of being prepared to die for him or her, should the need arise.

Third, the Focolarini teach that Christian love should

always give itself immediately it sees a need. It shouldn't wait, like human love often does, until it has assessed all the consequences of what it is doing. It should be immediate, spontaneous and concrete. Otherwise we tend to neglect the opportunity to love in the present moment. We think of all sorts of reasons why we can't love. We forget that only the present exists, and that if we want to love we can only love now. We put things off until the future – which for all we know may never come – or we retreat into the past, into our memories or dreams or regrets and do nothing, while life slips by.

Fourth, Christian love should always be supremely active. The Focolarini say that as Christians we should always love first. We should take the initiative and look for opportunities to heal and reconcile, to laugh with others when they laugh, and cry when they cry. Wilson Carlisle, who was founder of the Church Army, once said: 'Go for the worst.' Go, don't wait for events to come to you. And go for the worst; go for the cross, go to where there is darkness and suffering and try to heal it. Even if there is pain and suffering inside you, use it if you can to trigger off another little positive act as Jesus did when he was dying on the cross, where he summoned up his last strength to forgive the thief and ask his disciple John to look after his mother.

What had impressed me so greatly about the Focolarini was that they were actually loving like this in their daily lives. It was inspiring to feel their love and to witness their countless acts of sacrifice for others, their unconditional giving, and their immense faith which could move mountains. I felt that they lived in a world quite different from mine: a glorious, noble, heroic world which brought out the very best in each person. I felt that their world was a foretaste of heaven on earth. Also, while experiencing it, I could identify with many of the phrases, stories, incidents and observations in the Bible which before had appeared opaque or Utopian. I could also understand why the church had survived so long, and it was not because of the quiet charm of the English churches, nor the comfortable rituals of the Sunday services, as I had previously supposed. These latter were simply the dying embers of a blazing fire of Christian love – the living church – potentially capable of transforming the world.

The vision of love and unity realized in practice by the Focolarini did wonders for my morale. Just to be able to be with them made me feel alive again. It stretched my soul and I felt nothing was impossible. Yet I wasn't at all sure whether I was capable of loving like that myself. The demands on my ego were too great. I wasn't a saint, to put it mildly. Yet on the other hand the attractiveness of the way of life of the Focolarini was undeniable. I needed no further proof that if everyone would live like that all the problems of the world would be solved, all wars ended, all famines and disease obliterated. I had no alternative but to try it out for myself.

When I complained to the Focolarini that their regime of love was too hard for ordinary mortals like me, to my surprise they agreed. But, they said, Christian love doesn't derive from ordinary mortals. On our own, all our attempts to love will fail miserably. The Focolarini told me that I could only succeed in loving if I turned into a reality Jesus' promise that 'When two or three are gathered together in my name there I am amongst them.' They said that when Jesus is among us we experience a tremendous influx of spiritual energy which gives us the strength to love so intensely. What is more, we experience his presence with intense joy, like the disciples on the way to Emmaus.

How simple and yet how profound is the secret of the Focolare movement! They love by having 'Jesus in the midst'. Chiara Lubich, their founder, puts it this way:

> We know the answer: we have Jesus in our midst if we are united in His Name. This means that we are united in Him, in His will, in love which is His will, in mutual love which is the supreme will of Jesus, His command, where there is unity of heart, of will, and of thought, if possible in all things but certainly in matters of faith.
>
> *Chiara Lubich, Jesus in the Midst*[1]

Chiara also describes her own experience:

> I remember one day I was alone in the first Focolare house. I was preparing dinner. Through someone's lack of virtue before each had left for work, we did not part in full unity.
>
> I found I couldn't understand anything any more.
>
> I couldn't see the reason for the many sacrifices I had made to follow Jesus, such as leaving my family whom I loved so much. I couldn't see the reason why

I had abandoned so many things for him, like my studies for example. At one point during the day I was up in the attic getting wood for the fire, and I caught sight of the boxes of books I had loved so much. I remember the tears which fell onto the dust that now covered that previous love of mine, and I decided to wait for my friends to put Jesus back in our midst, so I would be able to see again. And that's what we did. When we were united, on the other hand, we felt all the strength of Jesus among us. It was as if we were all clothed in the power and blessing of heaven. We felt capable of the noblest actions for God, the most ardent, difficult resolves, which we subsequently maintained, whereas before when alone, for all our goodwill, it was difficult to fully live up to the promises we had made to the Lord. We felt a power that wasn't merely human.

Chiara Lubich, Jesus in the Midst[2]

The important spiritual insight from this story by Chiara was that one could go towards God together with others. Up to then I had always believed that the spiritual journey was essentially a one-to-one encounter with God. Treatises on the spiritual life, such as those by the Eastern Church Fathers, St Bernard, St Ignatius, St Theresa and so on, had all emphasized personal devotion and self-denial as the true path to salvation. For me this was somewhat dark and depressing. I was (and am) not cut out for a hermit's life! Excessive introspection can be a lonely pastime, and I had already had enough of that in my youth. The Focolarini gave me a quite different perspective, a way to God which was alive with active love for one another within the world and one which allowed one to share the spiritual journey with others, whilst also helping to heal the wounds of society.

The developments in my spiritual life originated by the Focolare at first all but buried the intellectual pursuits which had earlier seemed so important. If Christian love and prayer could conquer all things, provided one actually practised them, why bother with anything else? And if they were the keys to living life in general, they were assuredly also the key to work, which I was still very interested in understanding more fully. So I turned again to the Focolare for guidance. What did they say about work? I had already found out that a variety of trades were carried out in the Focolare village of Loppiano, so I thought that perhaps I might find some clues there about the spiritual significance of work, and a proper Christian way of carrying it out.

In the early days of Loppiano there existed several types of work. There was a vineyard, a pottery and arts centre, a caravan-manufacturing unit, an electrical repair shop and a rag-picking operation. I wanted to know what, if anything, was especially Christian about the way they carried out their work. It was the rag-picking operation which excited my curiosity the most, because it was the most meaningless. A large textile manufacturer was supplying Loppiano with tons of scrap cloth, waste rags – of different sizes and colours. The work consisted of sorting through these rags, separating them into their different colours, and then returning them to the manufacturer for further processing. The staff involved were placed in long rows with piles of mixed rags in front of them, and had to sort each colour into separate baskets. It was back-breaking work, carried out hour after hour, totally uncreative and requiring constant attention. It was not dissimilar, I reflected, to the rows of office desks I had encountered in my first job in Glasgow.

When I enquired as to what was especially Christian about this work – and the other work at Loppiano – I was given a refreshingly simple answer. The important thing, I was told, was to love one another to the point of being willing to lay down one's life for the other. The work was meaningless, it was true, so doing it caused a little suffering. The model of living in suffering was Jesus on the cross. His love for humanity was the greatest when on the cross he said 'My God, my God, why hast Thou forsaken me?' Just so, when we experience suffering, whether in rag-picking or when we see a poor, ill person, or whatever, we share in a cosmic sense Jesus' pain. Then, just like him, we must love the more, allowing the suffering to trigger us into a greater love.

Observing the rag-picking, I could see that this indeed was what was going on. People were trying to help one another, encourage one another, and serve one another because of those difficult circumstances. I was impressed but – I have to admit – I felt a little uneasy as well. It was one thing to love one another, but another to acquiesce in the meaninglessness of the work. Something was missing. Later, on a subsequent visit to Loppiano, I discovered what this was and what the Focolare were doing about it.

CHAPTER 4

A Collection of Theological Clues

Our amateurish efforts to emulate the Focolarini's practice of spiritual love taught Diana and me many things including, for example, a deepening understanding of biblical texts and the importance of regular participation in the Eucharist. This in turn led to a deepening of our prayer life. Our sense of awe and reverence for God's creation also increased. We were beginning to sense the unity between God, humanity and nature – an insight which was later to become crucial to a theological understanding of work and society. I remember when we went on holiday to Lake Vyrnwy in mid-Wales in 1969, writing down my feelings at the time.

I gazed from our bedroom window at the hotel at Lake Vyrnwy, over the wide still water onto the grey-green pines climbing up the hillside opposite. Slight swirling wisps of cloud drifted among the trees. A brown bird stood alone below the window in the gentle rain. A wasp settled on a wall tile a few feet away, sucking a trace of sweetness, I imagine. God, I asked, show me your presence in this peaceful scene. Everything seems to be calling to me that You are everywhere, in all the trees, the rhododendron bushes, the grass, the lake, the mist, the sky. But you, Lord, are veiled. I feel your presence, but I cannot perceive it. Please open my eyes.

And, most gracious Father, in your infinite gentleness and kindness, you helped me understand a few things. I saw how you had put the sweetness there for the wasp, and the wasp for the bird, and the bird for the trees, and the trees for the lake, and how all nature was interrelated in a beautiful, delicate and miraculous harmony. And I saw, too, how you had made all this for mankind, for me and all the world, out of love for us.

I knew it was for mankind because I could see from the window how we human beings were able to dominate the landscape, and also because I could see no one on earth to equal mankind. Then I saw how each part of nature, according to its different capabilities, ministers to a different need of man. Indeed, the thought came to me that nature in its several parts corresponds to man's several parts, in order that man's needs can truly be satisfied.

Interestingly, I discovered later that similar sentiments (only far better expressed) were to be found in the writings of the great Catholic philosopher and theologian Etienne Gilson. He holds that there is a hierarchy in nature in which each species surpasses the preceding one in perfection by the addition of newer and richer forms of being. He suggests that each more noble species absorbs the lower into itself so that it contains in a single union all that is inferior to it. The inanimate is in the vegetative, the vegetative is in the sensitive, and the sensitive is in the rational.

> Just as the triangle is in the tetragon, the tetragon is in the pentagon. The pentagon contains virtually the tetragon because it has all the tetragon has and more. But it does not have it in such a way that what belongs to the tetragon can be distinguished separately from what belongs to the pentagon. Similarly the intellective soul contains virtually the sensitive soul, since it has everything the sensitive soul has, and more. But it does not have this in such a way that it is possible to distinguish two different souls in it.
>
> *Etienne Gilson, The Christian Philosophy of St Thomas Aquinas*[3]

I had good reason to be grateful for these insights which came later to form a crucial part of my understanding of 'whole' work.

At the time, however, and amidst the tranquillity of the misty Welsh hills, I was unconcerned with philosophy. My soul was stirring. I sensed God in the fresh grass, in the remoteness of the place, in the calm cold mass of water that now covered the valley to form the lake-reservoir. There was once a village in the valley. It's gone now, except for a church spire protruding defiantly above the surface of the lake. In my mystical mood I read all sorts of messages into that bizarre symbol.

I had another experience at Lake Vyrnwy which has remained engraved on my psyche, and which was later to have a great significance in my theological understanding of modern work forms. I was sitting peacefully on a bare hillside overlooking the hotel on a slightly raw grey afternoon. Diana had stayed in the hotel below. Suddenly, without warning, I felt terribly afraid. I was pierced by a prickly sensation of intense evil. The source of the evil was behind me, over my left shoulder. I made myself look around, but saw nothing on the bare slope. Yet the feeling was so strong that I decided to get up and hurry back to the hotel. I felt I was about to be murdered! Then, all of a sudden, from the very place where I had felt such evil, there arose an immense shrieking and squawking, and a large flock of crows dashed as a body into the sky. Where they came from and where they went I do not know. But the feeling of evil immediately passed, and I was left utterly alone on the hillside, my heart beating wildly. I had known vicariously since World War II that there was evil in the world; now I felt it personally. Later I was to recognize it in the world of work.

As time passed, and the emotional experiences at Lake Vyrnwy began to fade, old intellectual preoccupations kept reappearing. I still felt a compulsion to know with my mind more about God's relation to his creation, and especially to understand better the Christian meaning of work as it had developed in today's modern industrial society. I resumed reading, mainly on the train to and from my office in

London. The starting-point was: What does the Bible have to say on the subject of work?

I soon discovered that several writers had already thoroughly researched the scriptures (particularly the Old Testament) for references to work. Their gist was well summarized by the Reverend Paul Ballard in a booklet written for the Industrial Committee of the Council of Churches for Wales in 1982. He concludes that although the Bible is the foundation document for the Christian tradition, all that can be found in it about work is a number of random and sometimes contradictory themes and references.

At an historical level, the Bible records the development of work patterns in the tribes of Israel as they developed from the simplicity of nomadic life to the more sophisticated structures of the monarchs and occupying powers. However, as Ballard points out, simply to follow the historical development of work in the Bible is insufficient and out of its contemporary context. The Bible is more than history since it tells the story of a covenant community which is under obedience to God and so is expected to live under God's law. Work is thus to be understood primarily in its relation to the covenant. This applies equally to work among the community of the Jews of the Old Testament and the Christian community of the New Testament, in whom the covenanted relationship with God was recreated through Jesus Christ.

Ballard goes on to investigate the nature of the covenant. He argues that its purpose is to fix the fundamental relationships between human beings and God and in principle this includes work relationships as well as personal relationships. One must therefore work according to God's law. The question is: what is God's law in relation to human work?

Ballard begins the search by taking God's work as the model for human work. God 'works' since he is creator of the world, of nature and of humankind. God works in that he gives form and power to all living things and sustains them in existence. God's creative work will be brought to completion when sin is overcome and all things are brought into his glory in fulfilment of his plan.

Although God's work is unique, Ballard maintains that human beings can enter into a creative partnership with him in terms of their own power over creation. So what does the Bible say about the daily work of Jews and Christians? First, Ballard observes that the Bible does not talk about fashioning the structures of the world as they exist today, but rather is interested in describing the attitudes to work necessary to assist redemption. Thus Paul, for example, warns Christians not to neglect daily toil since idleness is dangerous, and work gives a witness to others. Work also offers the Christian the opportunity to exhibit life in the Spirit since it facilitates the practice of patience, suffering and the sharing of the burden of the world. We work not for ourselves but for the common good in building up the body of Christ. Hence the Bible emphasizes the concept of vocation in that our calling to be in Christ requires special tasks to be undertaken which are described as 'gifts of the Spirit'.

On the other hand, there is the reality of sin, and the

Bible also speaks of work being a burden, a battle against nature and an occasion for obtaining riches at another's expense. Work in this context is understood as unlawful striving. 'What does a man gain by all his labour at which he toils under the sun?' (Ecclesiastes 1:3, NIV). Yet the Bible also speaks of the day of rest as both a practical necessity and a foretaste of the completion of God's work in creation. Finally, the Bible points to the relationship between work and faith. While preaching justification through faith, the Bible also makes it clear that work is a sign of faith and that without it faith is empty. Both faith without work and work without faith are useless.

The conclusion that Ballard draws from his survey of the Bible is that work has to be understood in a much deeper context than as a necessary daily activity. He says 'The power to work is a God-given power that finds its place in relation to the service of God and man's place in creation;' and adds 'but it is also the power for man to set himself over against God, to destroy creation and to turn human community into constant fear and strife and selfish greed.' Work in short is ambiguous and reflects the ambiguity of the human situation. It has a double nature: negative as a result of the fall, positive because through work man is a co-creator with God.

I must admit, interesting though these observations were, they didn't do much to help me find an answer to the fundamental questions which had been gnawing at me since I was a young man. Work was possibly the most powerful shaper of our industrial society. Surely one would expect the Christian faith – the Bible, the word of God himself – to tell us how our work, and hence society, could be redeemed! I was still hungry to find some practical help; it was not enough to be told that work 'reflected the ambiguity of the human situation'. I wanted to know how human work could be made God-like. So I went on reading and soon discovered that the ancient biblical themes had been refined and developed by the time of the Middle Ages.

A scholarly account of the medieval view of work is given in Edgar De Bruyne's book *The Esthetics of the Middle Ages*. (In using the word 'esthetics', De Bruyne was following its contemporary meaning in which the notion of 'work' is included.) The starting-point for the medieval scholars was that man is made in the image of God, and the universe is made in the image of man. Man, being a microcosm, reflects the harmonies of the universe, and the harmonies within God. 'The beauty of the circumscribed creature gives us an understanding of that Beauty which cannot be circumscribed,' as Isidore of Seville put it. This can be generalized by saying that all that is physical is a reflection of the spiritual; that the proper structure of objects in the natural world is analogous to the structure of the spiritual world. I could empathize with this view since I remembered how at Lake Vyrnwy I had felt how each part of nature was perfectly proportioned to the other.

As I explored these themes further, I found that similar ideas were being expressed by writers from different religious traditions, both within and outside Christianity. Frithjof Schuon, René Guénon, Seyyed Hossein Nasar and

Ananda Coomaraswamy had identified similar ideas within Islam, Hinduism and Buddhism. Within Christianity, Etienne Gilson, Jacques Maritain, Dorothy L. Sayers and G.K. Chesterton, to name some of the more accessible writers, were strongly pursuing the same theme. All concurred with the premise of the medieval scholars, that creation somehow mirrored the creator; 'as above, so below'.

Their reasoning stemmed from the fact that all effects must in some way resemble their cause. If God caused the universe to be created, and there is nothing outside God, in a deep way the universe must resemble God. Of course, the universe, being finite, is not God, who is infinite. God will remain in full, perfect existence, long after the universe has completely disappeared.

I remember once trying to explain this asymmetric relationship to our six-year-old daughter, by comparing God's creation to a thought in her own mind. She had been given a rag doll called 'Big Dolly' to which she was devoted, but which had eventually disintegrated. I said to her: 'Imagine Big Dolly in your head. Imagine him so much that you can see the shape of his body, his arms, his clothes and his blue trousers. Now imagine him walking about and smiling at you. Imagine him so much that he comes to really exist in your head. Imagine him so much that you know exactly how every cell of his body works, how every thought he thinks pops up in his mind. Are you doing this? Now please don't stop imagining him, because if you do Big Dolly will disappear.'

Just so, I believe, God holds the universe in his infinite

mind, which is pure love. He creates and recreates continuously. Moreover, the continuous act of creation is God's 'work'. Consequently if, as the medievals would have it, 'As above, so below,' it surely follows that the way humans work can and should mirror the way God works. But how? I couldn't see any parallels between human work and God's work. The gulf between the cause and the effect seemed much too wide to bridge. I made a note of some of the differences.

The way God works	The way humans work
God creates from	Humans manipulate pre-existing matter
creates eternally	Human work is temporal
infinite	Human work is limited
rfectly	Humans work imperfectly
very good	Human work is often sinful
freely	Human work can be coerced
effortlessly	We toil
His work is wholesome	Our work is fragmented
His work is always a blessing	Our work is sometimes a curse

The question that these contrasting attributes was raising was 'Given these colossal differences, in what ways can human work possibly become more like God's work?' At this time I had no answers. I knew from my own experience in the steel industry and elsewhere that most modern work certainly did not mirror its divine exemplar. The Medievals had said 'as above, so below', but what was the true nature of the relationship? Many crucial elements in my understanding were still lacking. In a word I had reached a point of being completely stuck.

CHAPTER 5

Discovering God in Work

It was about two years after my questioning that an event occurred, simple and commonplace, yet in its own way so extraordinary that it changed my whole life. It was an insight so far-reaching that in a flash I possessed a glimpse of what I had been looking for such a long time, so unsuccessfully. I saw how human work could, in theory, mirror God's work.

I was standing in our study at home. It is a small room lined with bookshelves and furnished with a mixture of Moroccan and Persian rugs, Turkish cushions, an appliqué tablecloth from India and some African tribal artefacts. Above the door is a small brass-rubbing of the Holy Trinity which Diana made in a nearby church soon after we arrived. The room looks out onto the parish church on the other side of the road. People say that there is a special air of tranquillity and peace. At the time I was experiencing anything but peace. Despite all my reading, I was deeply frustrated at not being able to find the fundamental link between the immense and intractable problems of the industrial world, and the powerful and saving powers of a

God who created the world, who was love itself and who declared his creation to be 'very good'.

Suddenly an idea struck me. I needed to go back to basics, to start again at the beginning. Work: that was the clue. But what did the word actually mean? A dictionary lay nearby, so I thumbed through it and eventually found a fairly lengthy and diffuse definition which listed about twelve different meanings of the word. But the interesting thing was that I did not assimilate what I read. Instead I became conscious of a simple distinction between 'the work' (noun); 'to work' (verb); and 'working' (present participle). And suddenly a light flashed across my understanding like a blazing comet in the sky. I saw in the depths of my being God as trinity in work: God the Father in the noun 'the work', God the Son in the verb 'to work', and God the Holy Spirit in the present participle 'working'. For me this was a revelation. I understood for the first time how God as trinity was 'in' human work, right at its heart, in all its forms and manifestations. Although human beings did the work, God as trinity somehow inspired it, and gave us the grace to get it done. The medieval scholars were right that there was a real analogy between God's work and human work. What they had failed to articulate, however, was that God is trinity.

I could only guess at the practical implications of this insight. I felt I had been marked in my soul with a great truth, which I understood in principle but not in fact. Before I was searching for something but I didn't know what I was looking for. Now I was searching still, but with a strong sense of direction. God as trinity was the compass.

From now on I merely needed to follow it. It was rather like looking for someone's name, then going through a list of names until the right one appears, and then knowing it is the name one was looking for. Just so, little by little, I began to piece together the functions of the world of work which resonated with the trinitarian insight I had received. What a sense of discovery this was!

The insight that God as trinity is 'in' work was accompanied by another breakthrough, another decisive turning-point for me, although now it is commonplace. This time it was in the field of industrial psychology. I discovered an article written by two people called Robertson and Paul, who had carried out some experiments on redesigning work. They had redesigned some people's jobs so as to make them more meaningful, more interesting and more satisfying. One of the exercises they carried out was to look at the jobs of a group of office workers. I remembered that I once worked in an office with thirty people, and it had never occurred to me that anything could be changed in there: that one could actually redesign the documentation; put the desks in different positions; and deliberately create the conditions for more satisfying human relationships.

I subsequently discovered that a lot of research had already been going on in the same field. One of the great pioneers was the American psychologist Frederick Hertzberg. In his early experiments, Hertzberg had asked a large number of people in industry, 'What do you like best about your work and what do you like least about your work?' He found that they liked best things like 'challenge', 'recognition', 'social relations', 'doing something complete', 'having a sense of achievement'. Robertson and Paul had used these concepts to build jobs. In other words, they had deliberately created the conditions for jobs to be made meaningful – a process which is called 'job enrichment'.

Hertzberg's seminal insights into job enrichment had been developed further by other industrial psychologists also. One of these was a pupil of Hertzberg's called Scott Myers, who later became a practising manager and an initiator of change at the workplace at Texas Instruments, a big electronics company in the USA.

Myers had hit upon an idea of fundamental importance. He had taken some of Hertzberg's 'motivators' – those psychological attributes such as self-responsibility, recognition and so on which people found most rewarding in their jobs – and translated them from the world of subjective personal emotions to the world of objective structures and systems. For example, instead of talking about 'self-responsibility' (a psychological concept) he translated it into the concept of 'planning' (an operational concept). To feel self-responsibility, of course, one has to have control over the 'planning' of one's work. The 'inner' feeling is facilitated by the 'outer' function.

Scott Myers also set about objectivizing the other factors which Hertzberg had discovered were motivators of people. Soon, he realized that all the motivators could be expressed and summarized in a simple formula which had three components. To be motivating work had to be planned, executed and controlled (or evaluated) by the worker himself. All Hertzberg's motivators fitted neatly into this framework. There first had to take place a process of deciding what was wanted: the action had to be originated. Next the decision had to be implemented in practice. Finally the whole activity had to be monitored: an assessment had to be made as to whether the job had been done well or badly in relation to what was planned.

As soon as I saw the words 'plan, do, evaluate' I knew that I now possessed a vital key to understanding the mystery of the relationship between God and work. I remembered 'the work', 'to work', 'working'. The functions of planning, doing and evaluating within the world of work were analogous to the functions performed by the Father, the Son, and the Holy Spirit in the Godhead. Of course there was no question of the functions being the same: God's real inner life is infinitely richer and more powerful than its external expression in human work; nor did my current understanding of the words 'plan, do, evaluate' necessarily reflect their divine prototypes. The way many people define planning, for example, bears little relation to the 'originating' or 'envisioning' characteristics of God the Father. But at least there was a connection to be explored and refined. I set to work to find out more.

It was first necessary to understand as best I could the essential theological differences between the three persons in God, and then to transpose these relations to the world of work. I was acutely conscious of the risks inherent in the process. On the one hand one could fall into the trap of fundamentalism in taking too literally one's understanding of the divine relations and 'force-fitting' them onto modern work; but on the other hand, I didn't want to lose completely the connections between the 'structures' of God and the structures in work, for that would have annulled the entire relevance of the only part of Christianity which is different from all other monotheistic religions, namely the incomparable mystery of the Holy Trinity. So the hunt was on.

With some considerable trepidation I began the task of trying to understand a little bit of the theology of the Holy Trinity, feeling totally inadequate for this new, colossal venture. However, I found myself with a unique opportunity to learn what I needed. I was invited, unexpectedly, to become a member of the Industrial Committee of the Board for Social Responsibility of the Church of England. This was a group of clergy and lay people with strong links into the world of work, whose remit was to advise the General Synod on business matters. I was introduced to the Committee by a dedicated trade-unionist named Tom Chapman, who had spearheaded the successful opposition to a communist-led attempt to take over the biggest UK engineering union by ballot-rigging. He was a fearless and passionate man of principle, who did an immense amount of good at no small personal cost. The scar across his rugged face was inflicted by some thugs he opposed.

Once on the Industrial Committee, it was not very long before I became tuned in to the ecclesiastical network and discovered who were the current thinkers and practitioners in the field. By chance, too, there was an excellent Franciscan library, full of religious and theological books, a few hundred yards from my office at the British Steel

Corporation in London. I met a lot of people and also read copiously, especially the medieval doctors of the church such as St Augustine, St Thomas Aquinas and St Bonaventura, as well as some of the more recent theologians such as Rahner, Macmurray, Ott, Daniélou, de Lubac and the like. I found that the link between the Holy Trinity and human work, though completely overlooked by nearly everyone, was totally compatible with the treasury of common Christian wisdom which was accessible to all believers.

The starting-point was to understand the key differences between the three persons of the Trinity. These are, in fact, expressed in the commonly accepted tenets of faith professed by all Christians in the creeds. The first part of the Athanasian Creed tells us precisely in what ways the three persons are different from each other and in what respects they are the same:

The Father is made of no one, neither created nor begotten.

The Son is from the Father alone, neither made nor created but begotten.

The Holy Spirit is from the Father and the Son, not made, nor created, nor begotten but proceeding.

So there is one Father, not three Fathers; one Son, not three Sons; and one Holy Spirit, not three Holy Spirits.

And in this Trinity there is nothing for or after, nothing greater or less; but the whole Three Persons are co-eternal to one another, and co-equal.

From the Athanasian Creed

If one studies this text carefully, one can see first of all that the Father and the Son are totally identical except in one respect: the Father is the originating principle of the Son. That is to say that the Father *is* the substance of God viewed as *origin*, and the Son *is* the same substance, but viewed as the indwelling *image* or *expression*, begotten of the Father. The Father is the fount, the ultimate primitive origin of God, while the Son, who is equally God, proceeds immanently from the Father within the Godhead as 'a spotless mirror of the working of God, and an image of his goodness.' (Wisdom of Solomon 7:26, NRSV)

The Creed then states that the Holy Spirit has a different relationship to the Father than has the Son since Christ is referred to as the only begotten Son, whereas the Holy Spirit is said to proceed from the Father and the Son. The church has always understood this to mean that the Holy Spirit is breathed forth by the Father and the Son together, as the empathy, energy, fragrance and sensitivity of the love through which they personally love each other. This is not to be confused with the essential love which is God's nature itself according to the words 'God is love'. Rather it is the quality of holiness of both the Father and the Son by which they relate to each other. Or put another way, the Holy Spirit is the vital action and energy by which their mutual love is made expressive. Also, as it is in the nature of love to give itself totally to the loved one, the Holy Spirit has always been known as a perfect gift.

The same relationships existing between the Father, the Son and the Holy Spirit within God are to be found in the work of human beings since 'God made man in his own image and likeness'. The theological arguments justifying the linkage are somewhat technical and so they are not readily accessible to the non-specialist. One has to navigate one's way through the differences between the one nature of God and the three persons; through the real relations and missions; and through the concepts of begetting, proceeding and spirating. One also has to understand the difference between the *ad intra* and *ad extra* operations of God and the fact that the three persons can be distinguished (through the appropriations) but not separated in creation. After this one has to follow those theologians who have tried to define precisely the nature of the relationship between God and creation, and who have demonstrated that it is quite legitimate to use various forms of analogy (such as the analogy of proper proportionality) to justify the resemblance of creation (as effect) to God (the cause).

It is not the place in this book to recount all these arguments, but let me just say that they confirmed that the links I was looking for between God and work were indeed fully and completely validated by the Church Fathers, by mainstream theologians, and by most modern leaders of the church. Having accepted that there is a linkage one can begin to tease out its implications. First, it follows that a person cannot reflect the Father in work unless he participates in the original act of envisioning the object he wishes to make, thus reflecting the Father as Ultimate Origin. That is to say the creative idea must emanate from the worker – the intuitive act of the imagination which precedes the fashioning of the actual material. It follows that the worker must also have the freedom to enable his idea actually to be executed. In other words he should possess power such as puts him in a position of a decision-maker who is fully authorized to originate or 'plan' all aspects of the work.

Turning to the Son, we can similarly see from the theology of the Trinity that he is the archetypal cause of the 'do' component of human work. He executes his Father's plan, he 'exteriorizes' it, he incarnates it within the bonds of matter, time and space, in its flowering or concrete individuality, from the moment of its conception until its final completion. He gives to work its full expression, everything that it is. The Son is the living embodiment of his Father's ideas as they exist and unfold in work. Metaphorically speaking, if the originating seed is especially the work of the Father, its expression as the tree is especially the Son's, as being the realization of the seed.

Finally, the Holy Spirit freely offers to each worker the skills, judgment and motivation which draws the work onwards from its origin to its final maturity or completion. The Holy Spirit continually guides everything to its fitting end, constantly evaluating, communicating, leading, counselling, uniting; causing each thing to unfold unerringly in a manner which befits its essence as originally conceived by the Father and revealed by the Son.

The Athanasian Creed also states that 'in the Trinity there is nothing greater, nothing less than anything else. The entire Three Persons are co-eternal and co-equal with one another'. From this it follows that for human work to be truly 'whole' the action of the Father in it should be coextensive with that of the Son and of the Holy Spirit. In other words 'planning' should be coextensive to 'doing' and 'evaluating'. Workers should not 'do' more than they can 'plan', nor should they 'plan' more than they can actually do. Proprietorship, that is ownership without involvement, is tantamount to making the Son less than the Father, which destroys the 'wholeness' of work.

These were heady ideas. The more I studied the theology of the Holy Trinity and creation, the more I was convinced that the analogies between the trinity in God and the concepts of 'plan, do, evaluate' in work were not simply metaphors but that they were founded on a real relationship. And then, to crown it all, I discovered a fascinating passage from one of the greatest of the Church Fathers which corroborated my thesis. You cannot imagine how pleased I was to find out that the great saint and doctor of the church, St Bonaventura, had already articulated the real relationship between the Holy Trinity and work in his masterpiece, *De Reductione Artium ad Theologiam* in the second half of the thirteenth century. St Bonaventura wrote:

If we consider the Method, we will see that the produced artefact comes forth from the maker by means of a similitude that exists in the mind. The maker plans before making an object, and then he makes the object as planned. The maker produces an external work as close to the internal similitude as he possibly can... Understand, accordingly, that no creature proceeds from the supreme Maker except through the eternal Word 'In whom he disposed all things'... and so, considering the illumination of mechanical arts in terms of the method of the production of the object, we see there the WORD BEGOTTEN and Incarnate, that is, the Godhead and humanity, and the complete range of faith.

St Bonaventura, De Reductione Artium ad Theologiam[4]

To obtain such explicit endorsement from such an impeccable source gave me renewed enthusiasm to search further. The next question was whether jobs which contained a full measure of planning, doing and evaluating were more motivating, satisfying and efficient, in other words, more 'whole', than those which didn't. I figured that if God was 'good' the closer work was designed to reflect God's trinitarian structure, the 'better' the work ought empirically to be. In the British Steel Corporation there was plenty of opportunity to find out.

CHAPTER 6

Scientific Verification

I had just been appointed to the post of Manpower Research Officer in the personnel department of the British Steel Corporation. The job was to develop manpower policies in order to increase the effectiveness of work in terms of efficiency and job satisfaction. The job came about in the following way. One day I had shared my enthusiasm for 'job enrichment' with an old colleague from Iron & Steel Board days, Pat Harlow. A few days later Pat came back to me and said he had found out something which might be of interest. Apparently the Manpower Research job had been advertised some time earlier but I hadn't seen it. There had been a long list of applicants, interviews had taken place and the job had been offered to someone who had subsequently turned it down. Pat asked if I would be interested in moving from corporate strategy to the job in the personnel department, since it might be a good place to find out more about people and their work. Although the job was relatively junior, I went to see the manager, we talked for ten minutes and he offered me the post without any further ado. This was quite unusual, since

I had no qualifications nor experience in manpower research techniques. It turned out to be a decisive move from the point of view of my researches. I couldn't have been luckier.

Bill Shaw, my boss, was a mostly gentle and kindly man who left me almost free to pursue my own interests as I thought fit. I was even given a budget and told to employ the best consultants and academics I could find to help with the research which British Steel felt was important to them. I was also exceedingly fortunate that the British Steel Corporation housed a very efficient library, run by a formidable lady called Miss Hook, who spared no effort to find me every obscure treatise on psychology, sociology and organizational theory I cared to ask for. She could even obtain books on theology and philosophy. I remember once asking her to find me a paper on Aristotle's Categories of Being, which she unearthed from an Irish monastery near Dublin.

Even more providential was the sudden arrival of a young man in my office one day, who was studying for a PhD in work organization and who wanted to attach himself to the British Steel Corporation in order to carry out a case study. His name was Roger Maitland and we eventually spent five extremely fruitful and constructive years together, researching every aspect of the subject of work. Roger had an encyclopedic mind, and an uncanny ability to find research from all kinds of sources in Europe and the USA. To cap it all, we had access to every steelworks in the British Isles to carry out field studies. I was also given the opportunity to go to the USA, Norway,

Sweden and elsewhere to learn from the 'gurus' of the day. We were incredibly privileged to have at our disposal better facilities than could be obtained in most universities, more freedom to pursue our own work, and access to sites for experimentation of which other people would have been very envious.

Our first experiment took place in the soaking pits at the Bilston Steelworks in the Midlands. Roger and I worked with a clever researcher from the British Iron and Steel Research Association named Keith Bibby, who had devised an ingenious way of measuring job satisfaction and its constituent elements. Each of the soaking pit operatives was interviewed, their responses ranked and then compared with other 'benchmark' jobs. From this procedure the prime determinants of job satisfaction could be determined. The results were exciting. The three factors at the top of the ranking list were 'control' (defined as the degree to which the person doing the job determines what he will do, the procedures by which he will do it, the pace at which he works, his freedom to leave the job, take rest, etc.); 'distinctiveness' (defined as the degree to which the job is a complete one, and significant in its own right, rather than an insignificant part of a larger process); and 'definition' (defined as the degree to which the purpose of the job and standards of performance were specified). The close correlation with our own categories of 'plan, do and evaluate' was striking, even though the terminology used was different.

The more we researched into work organization the more we were assured we were on the right track. With

Roger's help I collected a large amount of evidence from many eminent behavioural scientists, which showed again and again that when jobs included planning, doing and evaluating (in those days called 'controlling') components, they became complete and meaningful, and the work was improved both motivationally and in effectiveness. For example, we discovered that Lievegoed, the eminent Dutch behavioural scientist, had also noticed that 'complete jobs' were created when 'they include a certain amount of planning as well as execution and control'. Similarly, the American, Ford, had discovered that the enrichment of jobs involved improving work through systematic changes in three elements: the work module itself, which should be redesigned into a natural functional unit; control of the module, which should be given to the employee; and feedback from the module, which should also be given to the worker. Many others had reached similar conclusions. Marotta and Siderwitch showed that a job is meaningful when the individual is 'planning, doing and controlling a level of work which is commensurate with his work function'. Whitsett argued that an enriched job had three characteristics: first 'it is a complete piece of work' so that the individual can tell where his piece of work begins, where it ends, and in what way it is separable from the pieces of work of those around him; second, the job incumbent 'has as much decision-making control over how he is to carry out the piece of work as possible'; and third the individual 'receives frequent, direct feedback on his performance'. Again, Lawler and Hackman singled out each of these same components of meaningful work individually, and demonstrated that they were the key motivational variables in the work situation. Similarly, Poulson argued that 'we must create groups which may jointly plan, execute, control and complete any work assignment'. Again, Miller and Rice stressed both the feasibility and the desirability of requiring a workgroup to plan and execute a whole task. Finally, Foulkes concluded a review of the theory and practice of job enrichment by noting that, 'although many approaches to the problem of meaningful work were studied, it is noteworthy that similarities among them were greater than differences. In essence, all involved vertical job enlargement, or the addition of planning and controlling elements to the traditional "do" element of the job.' Foulkes' review was especially satisfying. It confirmed that science and theology were in agreement.

By this time I was also becoming more able to articulate (to myself anyway) the fundamental connections between Christian faith and work. The logic was simple. The Christian believes that man (male and female) is created in the image of God; God is a trinity; therefore man is created in the image of the Trinity. The three persons of the Trinity coexist in a dynamic relationship with one another, in that between them they constantly create, recreate and sustain the world. Likewise, as an image of God, human beings are free to co-create (i.e. work) in the same trinitarian manner. The relations within God are thus an ideal template against which we can compare the ideal structure of human work. The closer the resemblance to the trinitarian relations, the more 'whole' (holy) is the work; the less close the resemblance the greater the alienation, impoverishment and damage to human development in the work.

Yet I had the feeling that much was still missing from the analysis. There were flaws in the concept of job enrichment, not in its positive affirmations, but in what it left out. As we researched further, my suspicions increased. In particular job enrichment had two practical problems associated with it, which prevented it from becoming widespread in use. The first was that it failed to recognize that people don't usually work in isolation in modern work; they work with others. People collaborate to make a product or to provide a service. If one goes into a factory or office, one finds that the product or service is provided by a whole series of people, working together in an organization, each adding little by little to the product or the service. Most modern work is carried out within a system, by a collectivity. Job enrichment had ignored the 'systems' aspect. The danger of attempting to enrich individual jobs within a system was that one simply 'moved the furniture around'. A gain of some ingredient for one job too easily became a loss from someone else's.

The second flaw in job enrichment was that it did not directly relate to efficiency or effectiveness. Several attempts had been made to show that improved motivation generally leads to higher efficiency, but these were inconclusive. Consequently job enrichment had too often become associated with 'soft' or inefficient management. 'We are not here as a philanthropic society; we're here to make money,' was a typical reaction at the time.

It was thanks to a research body called the Tavistock

Institute in London not only that these problems were solved but also that the next theological breakthrough came. The Tavistock Institute will long be remembered in circles concerned with work organization for their phrase 'socio-technical systems'. They said, 'We mustn't only study work at the level of the individual; we must look at groups of people.' They also said, 'We can't ignore the task that the groups do; we have to look at technical issues as well as social issues.' So they brought efficiency and productivity into the equation.

At a stroke the Tavistock lifted the whole debate about job enrichment into a new arena, both from the point of view of industrial psychology and organizational theory and also from the standpoint of making Christian connections. New shafts of illumination began to dawn. In particular, I realized that to talk about groups of people automatically raises the issue of the relationships of people to one another. Relationships, in turn, are the subject matter of the Christian concepts of community and of the commandment to 'love your neighbour'. I recalled the Focolare's emphasis on 'Jesus in the midst'. By introducing the concept of groups another 'bridge' can be built which links organizational to theological concepts. We can begin to ask further questions such as 'Can the concepts of plan, do, evaluate be applied to groups as well as to individuals? Is it possible to organize work so that people can work together in small groups in such a way that they have both the opportunity and the incentive to make their own decisions, help, care for and support each other?'

In fact it is not only possible but also highly desirable to organize work in small groups in a modern work environment. Throughout modern industry the main unit of production has become the factory or plant, and the work processes inside them require close collaboration between people for the work to be done. The same applies in offices, hospitals and almost every other work environment. Hence there are good technical reasons, as well as social ones, why it is usually desirable to organize work so that people work in groups rather than as isolated individuals. In fact the evidence is that where people had been working on their own, and systems of group working are then introduced, for instance in the context of mass- and flow-production technologies, this has resulted in operational as well as behavioural benefits.

Research into small groups has been going on since the famous studies by Ed Mayo and others in the 1930s. It has been well documented and many experiments have taken place. I was able, with the help of Roger Maitland and Miss Hook of the British Steel library, quickly to assemble the relevant literature, including a mass of case studies trying to find out what makes a group function well.

One recurring theme which forced itself on our attention was the issue of group size. There seemed to be a consensus that, other things being equal, small groups are usually more effective, more friendly, more creative and more fun to be in than large groups. All sorts of evidence supported this contention from studies of fighting units in the army, to different sizes of classes in schools, to workgroups in industry, to the sizes which characterize most team sports. There was anthropological evidence too: the enduring presence of the hunting pack, the gang, the family, and several other similar-sized aggregations. I couldn't help adding to this formidable list the immensely significant small groups of Christians who met in each other's houses to break bread together, to help one another and to encourage one another to spread Christian love throughout the world by having Jesus in their midst.

Several reasons have been advanced as to why small groups are more effective than larger ones. They mainly centre on the fact that everyone in a small group has the opportunity to communicate with everyone else, while in larger groups there are too many interfaces to make good communication possible, so numbers of people get left out of the process and the large group eventually splits up into smaller cliques.

Attempts have also been made by behavioural scientists and others to quantify the optimum size of group as 'small'. For example, Miller and Rice place the optimum size of a primary workgroup at between eleven and sixteen people. Ketchum puts it between six and seventeen people. The Survey Centre of the University of Chicago, on the basis of problem-solving discussion groups held with over four million workers, advises that feedback meetings should not contain more than twenty to twenty-five participants. The Industrial Society recommends that for briefing groups 'there should not be more than fifteen to eighteen people, or there will not be that free interchange of question and answer which is so essential to achieve real understanding'. Other authorities have made similar estimates; and have argued that workgroups of approximately this size are essential to ensure both friendly and cooperative social relations between group members and that the group performs its collective functions efficiently and successfully. For my own work, I use the pragmatically determined size range of about four to twenty people, with the optimum size somewhere between these extremes, depending on the complexity of the work the group does.

To say that the basic organizational unit should be the small workgroup is not of course to imply that no organization should contain more than twenty people. Often several workgroups have to work together to achieve the larger purpose of the organization. For example in a bank, the army, a manufacturing establishment or the church, there are many workgroups connected together hierarchically, each contributing their little piece to the overall purpose of the larger organization. Perhaps wider organizations, as well as small groups, could benefit by being able to properly plan, do and evaluate their work?

CHAPTER 7

Work, Love and Theology

I can't remember exactly which year it was when we next went back to the Focolare village of Loppiano; it might have been 1975 or 1976. It had changed a lot since our last visit, becoming a centre of attraction for thousands of Christian pilgrims, both Italians and foreigners, as well as the simply curious who were moved by the living example of Christian love. Armed with my new theological insights about planning, doing and evaluating, and the benefits of small groups, I headed straight for the rag-picking, itching to see how it was progressing.

I was delighted with what I saw. The staff were no longer sitting in long rows sorting colours into baskets for eight hours per day. The whole layout and atmosphere had changed. First, they had reorganized themselves into small workgroups sitting in circles, so that they were close enough to help each other, share the work more easily and talk to each other. Second, they had rescheduled the working times in a more people-centred way. Third, they had broadened the scope of the work so that it included some further processing of the material, which called for greater use of their skills and abilities. In short they were, as a group, planning, doing and evaluating their own work. They were in control of the process. They were also monitoring and reviewing what needed to be done, how well they were actually doing, and what they could do to improve their work. They had migrated from an assembly line culture to an organization in which work was becoming more 'whole'. They were getting nearer to becoming a reflection of the Holy Trinity.

I celebrated inwardly. The Focolare were independently verifying the conclusions reached through theological and scientific research. It was fascinating to learn how they had done it, especially as I discovered that few of the people involved had knowledge of industrial psychology or organizational theory. Their response was the same as when we had met for the first time. They had simply tried to love one another to their utmost, like Jesus did when he was on the cross. Whenever they saw their neighbour struggling they tried to understand why, and then do something about it; if someone needed help but couldn't get it because they were seated too far away they moved the seats. Where they themselves experienced alienation or fatigue, they loved even more. Through the power of love and the spirit of service changes happened, and the work grew closer to the way God wanted it to be. Needless to say, effectiveness, satisfaction and any other parameters you care to mention improved as a result.

Although the visit to Loppiano touched me deeply in many ways, it left me with a nagging question. The Focolarini had dedicated their lives to unconditional

Christian love for one another before they made work (and by inference life) 'whole'. Love, not knowledge, was producing the desired results. They had succeeded because they were practising Christians. What concerned me was that by far the greatest proportion of the working population was not Christian. Was it possible, I wondered, to use theological insights to restructure work first, thereby making it 'whole' and then to rely on the positive effects of 'whole' work to gradually open people's eyes to more noble ideals, so that little by little they were brought to Christian love and belief?

Perhaps both routes were permissible: the way of love for the already committed and the way of theology and organizational theory for those who were not; love starting from faith, theology starting with the world as it is. Both ways had their attractions and their drawbacks. The problem with the way of love, as I saw it, was that it was likely to be permanently out of reach of the vast majority of ordinary people trying to cope with the vicissitudes of industrial or urban life, with its emphasis on materialism and individualism. It would take a massive miracle to convert a critical mass of humanity, especially as many of the people I encountered in my daily life had never even heard of the Gospels, let alone tried to live up to the exceptional demands of unconditional spiritual love. Did this mean that only a small minority of mankind could be saved?

The other way, however, was open to everyone. Yet it was much less pure and was quite capable of being subverted. Restructuring work successfully could just as easily make one wealthy as holy. Nothing I had discovered so far seemed powerful enough to guarantee permanent and profound changes in the behaviour of the workgroup. Through the way of love, group members automatically helped and supported one another. That commitment was made before the group was set up. But there was no such commitment in the way of theology. Restructuring work to make it 'whole' did not automatically bring people to want inwardly to collaborate closely with one another in the love of God. It could only remove external impediments which prevented people from so doing. Simply placing people into small groups, and giving them 'whole' tasks to plan, do and evaluate, might be a first step towards salvation, but it was certainly no more.

I was, however, determined not to give up. Much as I was trying to lead a Christian life of love at a personal level, I could not ignore the persistent call of my mind which seemed to be saying 'Go on with your researches: don't stop now. There are still more rich insights awaiting you.'

CHAPTER 8

Transformation through Christ

The next piece of the jigsaw puzzle that fell into place concerned the 'do' element of 'plan, do, evaluate'. I had been uneasy about the 'do'. Do what? The behavioural scientists had talked about 'a complete span of work', 'a meaningful job element', 'a natural module of work'. But nowhere was there a definition of what 'a complete span' actually contained, either at the level of the individual or at the level of the small workgroup. Was, for example, a thirty-second job cycle of an assembly line worker a complete span? Or did he have to make a whole product, or just a complete part? I did not yet possess any theological clues except that the 'do' element in human work was associated with the work of the Son within the Godhead. Then two things happened almost at once.

First, by chance I had picked up in a second-hand bookshop a dusty weather-beaten book called *The Christ of Catholicism* by Dom Aelred Graham, a monk of Ampleforth Abbey. Although written in 1947, it still stands as one of the most fruitful and lucid accounts I have ever read to explain Christ in his divine and human aspects. The book has chapters on the life and work of Jesus Christ, the personality of Jesus, Jesus as divine redeemer, and on the consequences of the incarnation through the ages. The pivotal section of the book is the explanation of how Jesus is both God and man, divinity and humanity harmoniously united.

Aelred Graham quotes Paul's beautiful passage in order to stimulate our wonder at the divine miracle of the incarnation of God as a human being. Christ, he said:

> being in very nature God
> did not consider equality with God
> something to be grasped,
> but made himself nothing,
> taking the very nature of a servant,
> being made in human likeness.
> And being found in appearance as a man
> he humbled himself
> and became obedient to death –
> even death on a cross.
>
> *Philippians 2:6–8 (NIV)*

In the book there is a precise definition of what is meant by the mysterious fusion of God and man – the 'hypostatic union' – and it explains that the one person of Jesus Christ has two natures, one of God and one of a human being. Graham also identifies the various heresies throughout the ages which have tried and failed to prove either that Christ was a mere man, or that he was only God.

As I read on, I was reminded of the medieval saying: 'as

above, so below': God's creativity in its 'eternal' aspect superimposed upon the world's finite specificity. Of course! Christ as God, Jesus as man: the 'God' part – eternal, archetypal, the model for humanity – shining through the human person of Jesus, a real human being who lived two thousand years ago in Palestine. So, if I wanted to discover how the Son could be a model for the 'do' part of human work, I would have to look to the manifestation of the divine in Christ, rather than his transient human and historical aspects.

The divine parts are eternal – valid for all ages; the human context had less significance for modern work. I was reminded of Ballard's observation that it was not sufficient simply to follow the historical development of work in the Bible, but that it had to be understood primarily in its relation to the covenant.

The other providential discovery also came through reading. I had long been an admirer of C.S. Lewis, whose many books I had both enjoyed and learned from. He was one of the few serious religious writers able to impart basic Christian truths without becoming either heavily boring or patronizing. His fluent, simple and catchy style made reading him effortless and fun. His messages were both refreshingly orthodox and memorable. Diana and I still talk of 'doing a Screwtape' when to please each other we both do something that neither of us wants.

I was reading and thoroughly enjoying one of Lewis's excellent books called *Miracles* when I came across a passage which inspired another vital clue to understanding the true nature of human work. C.S. Lewis had identified a crucial divine punctuation mark in Christ's mortal life and was relating it directly to nature. He is referring to the crucifixion and resurrection. He writes:

> It is the pattern of vegetable life. It must belittle itself into something hard and small and death-like. It must fall to the ground: thence new life re-ascends. It is the pattern of all animal generation too. There is a descent from the full and perfect organisms into the spermatozoa and ovum, and in the dark womb a life at first inferior in kind to that of the species which is being reproduced, then the slow ascent to the perfect embryo, to the living conscious baby, and finally to the adult. The pattern is there in nature because it was first there in God. All the incidences I have mentioned turn out to be but transpositions of the Divine theme in a minor key. I am not now referring simply to the Crucifixion and Resurrection of Christ. The total pattern of which they are only the turning point is the real death and re-birth.
>
> C.S. Lewis, Miracles[5]

I now possessed the vital clue which pointed to the relationship between God the Son and all natural processes, including work processes. If 'whole' work had to contain planning, doing and evaluating elements in order to reflect the Holy Trinity, the 'do' component had to contain a fundamental change of state analogous to the death and resurrection of Christ. The divine measure was nothing else than his death and rebirth. I marvelled at how obvious and elegantly simple was the connection. Come to think of it, there had already been various hints within the scriptures, but I hadn't seen their significance before. For example, Jesus himself said:

> I tell you the truth, unless a grain of wheat falls into the ground and dies, it remains only a single seed. But if it dies, it produces many seeds.
>
> *John 12:24 (NIV)*

Both my work within British Steel Corporation and personal experience confirmed that the same cycle of 'death and rebirth' characterizes all work processes, whether physical or otherwise. Anyone who has worked with raw materials can endorse this. For many years, for example, Diana and I used to bake our own bread. It is a wonderfully creative and therapeutic experience, and can produce delicious results. The process involves one, if not two, stages where undoubtedly a 'death and rebirth' of material takes place. The most obvious is the stage where the dough is put into the oven and the bread is baked. The dough 'dies' and the bread is 'born'. A real, substantive transformation of matter takes place; a sort of 'death and resurrection' in which the raw materials undergo a fundamental change of state, and emerge with new properties, functions, and even a new name.

Similarly fundamental or basic transformations occur in all authentic work processes whether in manufacturing, health, education or any other sector of society. They are to be found in iron and steel making, for example – the industry where I spent many years of my working life. The entire process, from extraction of iron ore from the ground to the production of the finished steel (the steel sheet or plate, bar or rod, wire or beam, or whatever) contains several key 'death and rebirth' stages, which are the centres of successive work systems. First, the rock deposits are turned into pure iron ore. Next the iron ore is turned into iron. The iron then becomes steel ingots. And finally the steel ingots are transformed into finished steel products.

In the health sector basic transformation stages are to be found within the variety of processes which turn a sick patient into a healthy person, or a pregnant woman into a mother and child, or even in a terminally ill person's journey to the after-life through the basic transformation of death itself. They are also to be found in educational processes, problem-solving processes, agricultural processes and administrative processes. Whenever work has to be done to turn one thing into another, certain basic transformations occur which are analogous to the transformation of Christ through his death and resurrection. At these stages, the factors of production (labour, machinery, materials, energy) combine to effect a quantum leap forward in the change process.

In physical production processes the possibility of carrying out these basic changes is determined by the laws of science, such as physics or chemistry. These laws are the most fundamental and unchanging aspects of any work. Any manager or engineer will tell you that basic transformations are the key conversion stages in a work process at which a substantive change takes place to the material or information being processed, and where the essential functional characteristics of the finished product are acquired for the first time. At a basic transformation stage in the process the inputs, in other words, raw materials or information, lose their identity; they disappear, 'die', are subsumed; and the product then acquires a new function, value, properties or purpose.

Because they represent the major change points in the process, there are usually only one or two basic transformations in the manufacture of a discrete product or processing stage. Basic transformations in a work environment are easy to recognize.

● They are the activities involving step-function or quantum-jump changes to the state of the product.

● They are often irreversible; what is done cannot easily be undone.

● They can be the most complex and difficult stages to control in a work process.

● They involve major physical, chemical, electrical, informational or other changes to the internal constitution or function of the product.

Basic transformations also represent the reason why other activities take place. They embody the purpose of all work processes, and are the place where value added is the greatest. Some examples of physical basic transformations (only at key conversion stages) include:

bake	fuse	mould
blend	granulate	oxidize
chlorinate	grow	polymerize
diffuse	hydrolyze	react
electrolyze	hydrogenate	saponify
extrude	ignite	solder
fire	laminate	standardize
form	melt	

What was becoming clear was that if human work was truly to mirror its divine exemplar, not only should small workgroups plan, do and evaluate their work, but the 'do' part should always contain a basic transformation stage which represented a 'crucifixion and resurrection' of matter.

I wondered, of course, whether these correspondences were merely metaphor and whether it was therefore legitimate to come to any generalized conclusions. It was. That the analogies were real was verified for me by three types of proof. The first was through a direct spiritual experience. At Lake Vyrnwy, I had become aware of the presence of God in all levels of creation as well as nature's ecological interdependence and subordination to mankind. Second, there was the testimony of respected theologians such as Etienne Gilson, who himself was carrying on a well-established medieval theological tradition, which also confirmed that 'as above, so below'. And finally I was to discover that these correspondences did in fact exist empirically; the facts proved it.

So far so good. But there were further parallels still to be made between Christ's life and the ideal span of human work processes to be undertaken by workgroups. C.S. Lewis had said that the crucifixion and resurrection, although very important, were only a turning-point in a total pattern. I was not yet sure what the 'total pattern' meant in the context of work, where it began and ended, although I anticipated that there would be synergy between the definition of a natural module of work (with a basic transformation at its centre), and a correct understanding of the 'total pattern' of Christ's life.

There was plenty of theological support for the integrated and mutually dependent nature of the stages in Christ's life. As all his actions were manifestations of the divine will, together they formed a 'whole' which gave each part its meaning and place in relation to each other part. The question was whether work processes demonstrated the same degree of interdependence of their parts so as also to form integrated 'wholes'.

The answer is that they do. Any manager or engineer will tell you that it is an inherent feature of all work processes that their constituent activities cluster around the basic transformation. The closer an activity is to a basic transformation, the more tightly causally linked it is to it. That is to say, the activities are highly interdependent or mutually in need of each other. Those responsible for designing work systems will further tell you that the causal links which bind activities together around a basic transformation in any work processes can be verified:

1. in the dovetailing of the technologies used at and around the basic transformation;

2. in the intensity of the information flow between the basic transformation and its supporting activities;

3. in the cause and effect chains caused by the instability or incompleteness of the product as it passes to and from the basic transformation;

4. in the exclusivity of customer–supplier relationships between the basic transformation and its neighbouring activities.

Once again science and theology are in harmony. There is indeed a close correspondence between process systems in the world of work and the 'total pattern' of Christ's life in terms of the close integration of component parts in each.

The 'wholeness' inherent in the divine again provides an accurate template for determining the 'wholeness' in the human. Chunks of every work process, in other words, form 'wholes' around various basic transformations in the process, just as the whole of Christ's life centred around, and drew its meaning from, his crucifixion and resurrection. I have come to call these complete spans of work 'whole' tasks. 'Whole' work is created when a small workgroup plans, does and evaluates a 'whole' task. In industrial language there then occurs a 'match' between the interrelations inherent in the social system (the workgroup) and the interdependences within the technical system (the 'whole' task). In theological language, the co-creation process (work), when made 'whole', exactly reflects the small Christian community meeting to celebrate the crucifixion and resurrection of Christ.

I also gradually came to see that the boundaries of any 'whole' task could be accurately determined by developing the analogies with the other specific points of divine intervention in Christ's life. In particular, the structure of work processes parallels those key points in his life, like the crucifixion and resurrection, where there had been explicit, tangible and clear-cut divine interventions, witnessed by several people, and carried out by one or other members of the Holy Trinity. There are six of these. First, there is the conception of Christ, since he was conceived by the Holy Spirit; second, the birth of Christ, since the glory of the Lord shone around the shepherds; third, the baptism of Christ, since the Father said 'Thou art my beloved Son' and the Holy Spirit descended as a dove; fourth, at the transfiguration, when the Father again said 'Thou art my beloved Son'; fifth, the crucifixion and resurrection; and sixth, the ascension, where Christ was seen by the disciples being raised into heaven. Analogous events to these points of divine intervention are embedded in all integrated work processes.

There is a beginning of every 'whole' task and this mirrors Christ's own conception. Any truly 'whole' span of work always embraces an originating aspect, a movement from non-being to being, and this divine marker reflects the fact. There are also striking parallels in work processes with the birth of Christ, in that there is always a moment in 'whole' human work when the original concept becomes materially visible for the first time. There are interesting parallels, too, with baptism in all 'whole' work processes. This is the first time when the raw materials come together in order to be transformed in the conversion process. Then there is the archetypal significance of the transfiguration – of the opportunity a workman should have to glimpse a vision of excellence in his craft. Next comes the crucifixion and resurrection which we have already discussed. Finally, a truly 'whole' task ends at the point of final completion of the product: an ascension into a new order of use, as it were. Each 'whole' task thus first contains a full preparatory stage where the materials are ordered, assembled and made ready, then come one or more basic transformation stages where the major conversions take place, and finally a completion stage where the final touches are added to perfect the entire product. When a small workgroup fully participates in all these stages, divine resonances appear in the work: it can be done more efficiently, it is more satisfying, it is more sustainable in relation to the wider community and it can stimulate the worker's voyage along the spiritual path towards God.

What a discovery this was! As C.S. Lewis said, transformations in nature are 'but transpositions of the Divine theme in a minor key'. What Christ, the author of creation, did once and for all, is the archetypal process which the entire universe must follow. To be 'whole', man

as co-creator must imitate in his human work the work of
the creator himself 'who came down from heaven, was
crucified, dead and buried, and on the third day rose again
from the dead'.

CHAPTER 9

Creating 'Whole' Work in Practice

There had already been plenty of opportunity in the British Steel Corporation, not only to research into 'whole' work but also to create it for real. I was closely involved in designing the organization and job structures in several of the new steelworks which were being built during the expansionary 1970s. Two prestigious examples were the new ore terminal at Hunterston on the west coast of Scotland, and the huge blast furnace at Redcar on Teesside. I couldn't help feeling a sense of destiny in the latter case since the blast furnace was called the womb of the industrial revolution, the very symbol of what I was trying to understand and change. Perhaps in a small way I was indeed taking part in the birth of a new Christ-centred revolution.

It was 'a small way' since we in fact only had a marginal influence on the creation of 'whole' work. The technical and political constraints under which we were working were so great that we could only slightly improve the design of jobs, let alone the design, layout and scale of the ore terminal or blast furnace themselves. The biggest obstacle to creating 'whole' work was the sheer size of the investments. The ore terminal occupied an area of several acres, criss-crossed by long stretches of conveyor belts, punctuated by huge cranes and the largest jetty in the UK. As a result many jobs were located in isolated parts of the site, which made it difficult to form cohesive workgroups. Also it was questionable whether there were any true basic transformations in the ore terminal, since it was really just a gigantic handling and storage operation. The Redcar blast furnace was similarly beset with technical design decisions which effectively prevented many 'whole' jobs from being formed. For example, the blast furnace was as tall as St Paul's Cathedral. In order to feed iron ore into it a conveyor belt had to be installed. It could not be too steep since otherwise the iron ore would slip backwards down the conveyor. A little mathematics showed that the conveyor belt had to be at least a quarter of a mile long. At its foot a steelworker had to be stationed to guard against blockages and breakdowns. His job was isolated, boring, unskilled and far removed from the basic transformation of ironmaking taking place in the blast furnace, which gave the whole enterprise its meaning.

When steel plants were not of such a huge scale, we were able to restructure work much more radically. An early exciting project was the restructuring of the finishing end at Bilston Steelworks – another part of the same site on which we had conducted our first survey of job enrichment. Having regrouped the labour force into small workgroups which could each plan, do and evaluate a 'whole' task centred on a basic transformation, everyone was delighted at the immediate improvement in efficiency and job satisfaction. I rejoiced that some 200 people were re-enacting each day an echo of the death and resurrection of Christ. There was restored a faint resonance with the divine, long lost within the meaningless mechanization of industry. I hoped that these chords of harmony might once again awaken people's sense of the eternal, spiritual rhythms of the universe, and perhaps bring them a little nearer to God.

Although proven success brought many other requests for help to reorganize work, there were many difficulties, not least at Bilston. In the mid-1970s, the trade unions in the steel industry were immensely powerful, and unfortunately some less-enlightened elements were resistant to any change at all. The implications for the rest of the Bilston site of the restructuring work in the finishing end were too much for the unions at the time, and an extension of the work to the rest of the site was resisted.

There was, however, a postscript to this story. Three years later, as part of the major retrenchment and down-sizing of the UK steel industry at the time, the Bilston works as a whole was closed down. I remember the occasion with sadness. My office in British Steel's Headquarters at Grosvenor Place, London, was on the third floor at the front of the building overlooking the grounds of Buckingham Palace. (Incidentally I never saw the Queen walking in the gardens, although helicopters took off and landed occasionally.) On the other side of the corridor to my office was the big committee room where the major national negotiations with the trades unions took place. The fateful day arrived when Bilston union officials were summoned to be told of the closure of their steelworks, the biggest employer in an area of high unemployment in the Black Country north of Birmingham. After the meeting the shattered shop stewards, some almost in tears, filed silently out of the committee room. Among them were the two shop stewards from the Bilston finishing end. When they saw me through the open door, they and the entire delegation came into my room. They thanked me for all the work we had done at Bilston, and then said with great emotion: 'If only we had listened to you and implemented your ideas over the rest of the site, we would not have had to shut down.' The whole delegation then shook me by the hand and departed. I was never to see any of them again.

Word, however, had spread around, and I was lucky enough to have had several other invitations to reorganize factories up and down the country. Paradoxically only a few were within the steel industry, due to the massive worldwide over-capacity which had forced British Steel into the period of large-scale closures – and a major strike – leaving attempts to create 'whole' work somewhat stranded. But opportunities outside the industries were beckoning. For example, David Pilkington, personnel director of Pilkington Glass, invited me to St Helens. I was also asked to reorganize the Carreras-Rothmans plant at Basildon, and the work structuring principles were then used to design their new factory at Spennymore, as well as contribute to the big Courage Brewery Plant near Reading by the M4 motorway.

Meanwhile, back in the Steel Corporation in 1979 the then chairman Sir Charles Villiers invited me to set up a new unit charged with reorganizing the industry on a much broader basis. When his proposal was debated by the Board, it was turned down on the not-unreasonable grounds that it was politically unacceptable for Head Office to set up a new unit at a time when they were shutting down so much of the industry.

With opportunities to expand my work elsewhere increasing, and work in British Steel declining, it was clear that the time had come to leave. With the full support and encouragement of Diana, my family and friends, and with grateful thanks to the industry where I had been permitted to learn such a lot, I left my office on 30 June 1979 for the last time, to begin a new career.

When I left British Steel, I was determined to put into practice a theology of work on as wide a scale as possible. Having been an 'internal consultant' at British Steel for the previous eight years, I thought that with the good contacts already made I could continue in the same vein as an 'external consultant'. For a time, however, fate had other intentions. I was unexpectedly offered, and accepted, the post of Seear Industrial Fellow at the London School of Economics. The job was a combination of teaching and research, and it also left time for some consultancy work. It was an ideal springboard from which to take the plunge from the relative security and privilege of a large nationalized industry to the uncharted, risky and, for me, frightening world of free enterprise. I was forty-two years old. I was also fortunate to have as colleagues at the

London School of Economics Professor Ben Roberts, Professor Keith Thurley (who tragically died in 1993) and Dr David Guest (now Professor Guest), all of whom were highly respectable academics in the field of personnel management and industrial relations. They gave me immense personal and intellectual support, and I owe them much.

During my two years at the London School of Economics, several consultancy opportunities presented themselves, notably with Philips Electronics, under the patronage of their technical director, Dr Leendert Weeda. We carried out major restructuring work in several of their UK factories in areas as diverse as TV tubes and sets, semiconductors, laser discs, wire filaments, metal components, magnets, and a multitude of electronic components. The theological principles were followed faithfully and, again, brought major benefits to employees and employers alike. I left the LSE in 1981 to begin a full-time consultancy career.

CHAPTER 10

The Mystical Body of Christ

During the same time that the notion of a 'whole task' was being developed, new crucial theological concepts were emerging. Their source was the Roman Catholic encyclicals. These are a series of pronouncements by a succession of Popes on the major ethical, ecclesiastical, political, social and economic issues of the day. They provide an excellent framework of principles for reflection and action. Of particular interest to me were the social encyclicals, beginning with the world-famous encyclical *Rerum novarum* written by Pope Leo XIII in 1891, since they touch on the subject of work.

I read them carefully: *Laborem exercens*, *Quadragesimo anno*, *Populorum progressio*, *Gaudium et spes*, *Mater et magistra*. These and the other social encyclicals contain an immensely rich treasury of wisdom, and should be mandatory reading for all Christians concerned with social issues. I will try to summarize some of the key points.

In the first place the encyclicals establish the right of the church to pronounce on social and economic questions. This is because scripture and natural law are the sources of the church's teaching. The encyclicals do not contain detailed answers to every social and economic problem, but they do point to the divine principles underpinning them. These principles, and the human rights which derive from them, are founded on the primacy given to the human being who is made in the image of God. It is fundamental therefore that all policies and economic processes should be shaped for human beings, and not the other way round. Vital principles safeguarding the primacy of the human being include the need for freedom as a basic value, and the supporting social principle of subsidiarity, which lays down that 'every social activity ought of its very nature to furnish help to the members of the social body and not destroy or obstruct them'. Subsidiarity ensures that higher authority and social institutions only take on tasks which cannot be satisfactorily carried out at a lower level.

Another vital principle emphasized in the social encyclicals is that of human dignity, which also stems directly from the view that every individual is made in the image of God. It follows that human beings possess certain inalienable rights to uphold their dignity, and these include working rights, such as the right to work, the right to humane working conditions and the right to co-determination and self-responsibility.

Another key principle advocated by the encyclicals is that the human person is a social being, since it is clearly stated in the creation account 'So God made man in his own image, male and female he made them.' From this comes the principle of solidarity, and the right to belong to organizations of one's choice, including trade unions.

However, since individual human freedom and dignity cannot always be reconciled with solidarity there is also a need for the protection of the common good, and this is ultimately a function of the state, supported by every citizen.

Yet another vital principle according to which all levels of society should regulate themselves is the principle of social justice. To work effectively, this needs to be infused with social love or charity, i.e. it should be a justice based on fraternity. Social justice also includes responsibility for all creation, including the environment.

These fundamental principles and rights underpin the Roman Catholic church's teaching on many issues of contemporary social and economic importance; issues such as property rights, the relationship between labour and capital, capitalism and the social market economy, Marxism and the class struggle, trade unionism and co-determination, strikes, entrepreneurs, the unemployed and a host of other topics which I had studied in my politics, philosophy and economics degree at Oxford many years before.

I have to admit, however, that I was slightly disappointed with what I had read, since I could find little about the New Testament notion of God as Trinity, nor of Christ's relation to work. The nearest the encyclicals came to my particular interests were in the references to the humanization of work. In *Mater et Magistra*, for example, Pope John XXIII says that 'every man has of his own nature, a need to express himself in his work and thereby to perfect his own being', but he doesn't go on to explain what 'expressing himself' means. Pope John Paul II writes in similar vein in *Laborem Exercens*.

On the other hand, none of the encyclicals I had so far read had concerned themselves specifically with the task of identifying the characteristics of 'whole' work itself. The social encyclicals were all about social and economic issues seen from a macro-perspective of principles and rights in law. Although I agreed with nearly everything that had been written it did not provide the practical guidance I was looking for, namely how to develop my understanding of 'whole' work for small groups of individual human beings. I had by then, in addition to the encyclicals, read everything I could lay my hands on about a theology of work: Chenu, Cox, Cronin, Todd, Preston, Temple, Munby, Welty, Queffélec, Savary, Wilhelmsen, Herr, Burckhardt, Fremantle, Gill, Mascall, Catherwood, Kane and Keiser, to name but some. I could find little more about the nature of 'whole' work either in the works or in any other theological bibliographies available at the time. Where else could one turn?

Then a breakthrough came. I chanced to come across another encyclical which had nothing to do with social policy, but which was concerned with the nature of the church. It was Pope Pius XII's *Mystici Corporis Christi*. The title was based on a simple definition of the church which had stemmed from the great medieval theological tradition, which in turn had its foundation in the early church of the first and second centuries. The church was called the mystical body of Christ.

'Of course,' I said to myself, 'how blind I've been.' By

focusing attention too narrowly on the work itself, I had completely overlooked the theological significance of the most human of all the elements of work, namely the workgroup. Up to then I had only observed the sociological importance of workgroup size and to a certain extent, of relations within groups. Yet here staring at me was a new treasury of theological insights. If the divine model for work is the Holy Trinity, the divinely designated model for the workgroup is the church: the church as the mystical body of Christ.

The way forward was now clear. What I had now to do was to uncover ways in which workgroups could be made to be more like their prototype, the church – not, of course, the historical church with its massive imperfections, but the church in its purity as an exemplar – as the 'spotless bride of Christ'. To be 'whole' the workgroup had, within its inherent possibilities, to bear the characteristics of being a 'body', of being 'mystical', and of being 'of Christ', just like the church.

The logic for equating workgroups with the church was simple. As the possibility of salvation is open to every human being, every group can, in principle, attain unity with Christ through the Holy Spirit. This was the inspiration behind the Focolare movement. Their unity is based on the reality of Jesus' promise that 'Whenever two or three are gathered together in my name, there am I among them.' Now when Jesus is present in a group – any group – that group is undoubtedly part of the church. But even if he is not fully present, the group remains potentially part of the church; the church in principle if not in fact. I therefore needed to find out how workgroups could be structured so that they displayed the same divinely inspired characteristics as the church, the mystical body of Christ.

CHAPTER 11

Designing 'Whole' Jobs

References to the church as 'body' were not hard to find. For example, Paul in his famous passage in 1 Corinthians 12 describes quite clearly what is meant by the church as body. He says:

> The body is a unit, though it is made up of many parts; and though all its parts are many, they form one body.
>
> Now the body is not made up of one part but of many. If the foot should say 'because I am not a hand, I do not belong to the body', it would not for that reason cease to be part of the body, and if the ear should say, 'because I am not an eye, I do not belong to the body', it would not for that reason cease to be part of the body. If the whole body were an eye, where would the sense of hearing be? If the whole body were an ear, where would the sense of smell be? But in fact God has arranged the parts in the body, every one of them, just as he wanted them to be. If they were all one part, where would the body be? As it is, there are many parts, but one body. The eye cannot say to the

hand, 'I don't need you!', and the head cannot say to the feet, 'I don't need you!' On the contrary, those parts of the body that seem to be weaker are indispensable, and the parts that we think are less honourable we treat with special honour.

1 Corinthians 12:12, 14–23 (NIV)

This statement has important implications for the desirable composition of any group. Paul is saying that if people are to help one another in a meaningful way, they should not be grouped together so that all members of the same group have identical roles. I wonder what he would have thought of a typing pool or a room full of lathe operators, or a football team comprised entirely of goalkeepers, for example.

Paul would have a lot of support from many managers today. Most would agree that multi-disciplinary teams containing all the core skills necessary to carry out their work successfully are in principle much more effective than groups whose staff are carbon copies of one another.

It is also worth noting that Paul speaks of 'an eye' and 'an ear' and not (if this doesn't sound silly) of 'half an eye' or 'half an ear'. The inference is that in Paul's view, the members of a body should themselves be doing something 'whole', and not be given arbitrary meaningless segments of work, as is often the case on an assembly line for example. The Christian notion of church as body implies that jobs should be functional 'wholes', along similar lines to those advocated by the job enrichment experts. Each job should thus contain a meaningful transformation which the job holder can plan, do and evaluate. With this formula, again, theology and the social sciences coincide.

In my own career I have seen many workgroups which have the characteristics of a body, and many which have not. I have also seen many 'whole' jobs, and many 'fragmented' jobs; and there is no doubt as to which are the most satisfying and efficient. Yet, strangely, workgroups containing numbers of identical and fragmented jobs are much the more common throughout industrial society today, for example in engineering, banks and hospitals. For reasons which would become much clearer to me later on, the notion of the workgroup as 'body' has been lost.

The fragmentation of work was exemplified in a washing machine factory I once reorganized. In the production area a typical assembly worker had only thirty seconds to assemble his portion of the washing machine before the conveyor belt whisked it away and another machine took its place. A typical job was to drill two holes, fix an electric cable (nothing to do with two holes) and screw on a bracket and some other unrelated bits and pieces. There were sixty-nine people on three assembly lines each doing similarly meaningless work. Where were the 'eyes' and 'ears' in that body? At the end of the line the washing machines were then tested by a different group of people from another department. Another body consisting entirely of 'eyes'! Not surprisingly they found 132 faults for every 100 machines passing through the testing station, and several more were undetected. Also the sixty-nine assembly workers were all in the same workgroup under a single supervisor – a giant body. There was a lesson here about the importance of small groups. I remember asking the supervisor how he managed to control such a large group of people. 'Easy,' he said. 'As long as I stay in my office they behave themselves. They only get stroppy when I go out onto the shop floor.' When we went out on the shop floor I saw what he meant. As soon as we were seen walking around, the assembly line workers started to bang their metal tools against their equipment in an intimidating show of defiance, like prisoners banging their tea mugs in their cells. The place was out of control, productivity was appalling, industrial relations and motivation were at rock bottom, and the company was on the brink of liquidation. Shortly afterwards, in another incident, the supervisor was sacked for fighting an operator, who was high on drugs. The only reason that there wasn't complete chaos was because the trade unions had a firm grip on the men – and on the company too for that matter. They had recognized the importance of the small group. There was a shop steward for every twelve people in the factory! Only when the assembly lines were so reorganized that small groups of people could plan, do and evaluate 'whole' tasks did the fortunes of the company improve.

It is worth digressing here for a moment to explain why long assembly lines with very short job cycle times for each worker don't work well. The problem is that it is virtually impossible to design work so that sixty-nine people each do exactly thirty-second work cycles (as in the washing machine example above). In reality some do slightly more and some do slightly less. Since the whole assembly line is limited by the slowest job stage, it means that there is an overall productivity loss. For example if some job cycles are twenty-five seconds and others thirty-five seconds, there is a productivity loss of up to 30 per cent since all the faster people have to wait for the slowest person to catch up.

Now imagine that the assembly line is replaced by four U-shaped lines of fifteen people in each, with each line making a complete washing machine. The job cycle time for each worker is now two minutes, and the same ten seconds delay only causes an 8 per cent productivity loss. If groups of three people were to have made the entire washing machine between them, the job cycle time would have been ten minutes each, with virtually no loss of productivity. The interesting point about these statistics is that they show in practical terms that when work is organized in a way which is closer to its divine exemplar, it is actually more efficient than when organized differently. It is also more satisfying. There is plenty of evidence to show that the longer cycle times are less fatiguing and stressful than very short cycle times. They also allow the work to be divided up into natural and meaningful 'whole' modules conforming more closely to Paul's notion of 'body'.

Actually – to finish off the story – the factory was later restructured so that small groups could make an entire washing machine and also test it for faults after it had been built (i.e. all the job holders carried out a 'plan–do–evaluate' cycle). The trinitarian wholeness of work was thus approached more nearly, efficiency and motivation improved dramatically, errors fell from 132 per hundred to 27 per hundred, productivity rose by 30 per cent and industrial relations and job satisfaction went up significantly. That part of the company was saved from the liquidator.

CHAPTER 12

True Leadership

The second element in the definition of the church as 'mystical body of Christ' which, when transposed to any group, has a defining influence on its effectiveness are the words 'of Christ'. It is not just a body, but one which belongs to and is governed by someone who is its leader. Christ is the head of the church as body; he was and is its leader, both during the time he was alive and after his death through the apostolic succession. Since the church is in principle available to anyone, it follows that leadership in a Christian sense is also in principle intrinsic to all groups. Expressed in the language of organizational theory, one can say that each workgroup should include a designated leader.

For most people familiar with the world of work this is a self-evident truth. But not for all. Lurking in the corridors of management theory is a view that workgroups do not need leaders. The theory is expressed under the pseudonyms 'self-responsible groups' or 'semi-autonomous groups'. Its liberal-minded proponents justify their theory, not on the basis of any rigorous scientific analysis, but on the belief that leadership is repressive by nature, that it stultifies the personal development of the led, and that it is a hallmark of an immature organization from which people should be liberated. This is a dangerous theory: it's quite untrue; it fails completely to understand the true nature and functions of leadership and, if applied, it eventually and paradoxically leads to dictatorship and slavery. Its proponents are incidentally managers who insist on personally being the boss of their own departments and are happy to sit on a management team with their director as leader, but who for some inexplicable reason don't believe that what applies to them is good for workers on the shop floor.

In the mid-1980s, I was invited to restructure the large Philips Electronics plant at Blackburn, Lancashire. Part of the remit was to reorganize the wire factory which made filaments for light-bulbs. It was an enjoyable and successful project, and I worked closely with the manager, Jimmy Saul. We turned a half a million pound loss into a half a million pound profit in three months, without reducing manning levels and greatly improving the lot of the workforce in the process. The significance of Blackburn was that it was in that very factory where one of the earliest and best publicized experiments in leaderless workgroups had taken place in the mid-1960s. It was hailed at that time as a great success, and had a not inconsiderable influence on management thinking, coinciding as it did with the liberation years of the Beatles and 'flower power'. Naturally, I was very curious to know the long-term outcome of the experiment, and I was particularly fortunate when I discovered that Jimmy Saul had been the very manager who had been asked to introduce it. Better still, he had kept the complete set of files relating to the work. What they showed, and Jimmy confirmed to me personally, was that the experiment had not been a success at all. Morale and productivity in the areas involved had fallen, and two years after its inception the experiment was abandoned. Apparently, the workers involved had sent a delegation to the management begging them to restore a leader. The main reasons were that the group could not handle conflicts among its members, and also lacked an advocate to represent their interests to senior management. It had become disenfranchised.

I have made a point over the years of carefully following the fortunes of 'leaderless' groups. In only one case were they what they appeared to be. Invariably there was a leader, if by another name. The one case I came across of a genuinely leaderless group was in the confectionery industry where, frankly, I was appalled at the prevailing work culture. First, the jobs were high-speed, repetitive, monotonous, stressful and totally prescribed by an intrusive technology; there was no margin at all for personal initiative or control. Second, there was no system of worker representation: the trade unions had been chucked out. Third, the conditions of employment were strict and unbending, with severe sanctions if they were flouted. And fourth, the pay rates were 50 per cent above the average in order to persuade workers to stay on in these conditions. It was, incidentally, also a white ghetto in a multi-racial area. I used the words 'dictatorship' and 'slavery' a couple of paragraphs ago. This example illustrates why.

The reality is that, in common with other theologically derived insights, the divine exemplar governs the human condition. Because Christ is the head of his body, the church, and any group is the church in principle, Christ is in principle the head of all groups. Since his death his leadership has been invested in designated human beings through the apostolic succession. Hence all groups should include a designated leader.

What are the necessary functions of leadership as derived from the analogies with Christ? Scripture teaches us that Christ displayed the kingly, the pastoral, the priestly and the prophetic functions. These same four functions happen to be precisely those which are the non-delegatable leadership functions in that they cannot sensibly be distributed amongst group members, but have to be performed by one person on their behalf. In the language of organizational theory, these functions are called the functions of high-level coordination (kingly), people development (pastoral), process champion (priestly) and management of change (prophetic).

I well remember an incident which beautifully illustrated these theological connections. I was involved in restructuring a large US-owned chemical plant in South Wales, my coordinator being their training manager, one Alastair MacDougal. Alastair did not entirely share my insistence that each group should include a designated leader, and we had several stimulating conversations on the subject. One day, on one of my regular visits to the site, Alastair cornered me and said triumphantly, 'You're wrong about leaderless groups. I have just proved that they are better than groups with a leader.' I asked how he had come to this conclusion, and he told me the following story. 'I hold' said Alastair, 'regular training courses for middle managers in the company. During the course we play a number of management games to teach certain skills, including a game to improve communication skills. For this game, I divide the twenty or so course participants into three groups, and I select a leader from each group. Before the game starts I take the leaders into another room and explain the rules of the game to them. Each leader and his team has to solve a problem. The nature of the problem and various clues associated with it are written down on a number of cards. Each leader is given an identical pack of these cards and told to go to his group, deal out the cards equally to each group member, and then lead a problem-solving session in order to find the solution to the problem. The rules are that no one is allowed to show anyone else in the group his cards except under the direction of the leader, when they are allowed to read out words on a particular card to other group members.'

'Normally', said Alastair, 'the average group takes about eighteen minutes to solve the problem. However, thanks to our conversations, I decided to carry out an experiment on the last training course. Instead of designating three leaders and managing the game through them, I decided to hand the cards out directly to each group and say to each: "Now here are the rules of the game, go ahead and solve the problem between yourselves."'

'Do you know', said Alastair, 'how long these leaderless groups took to solve the problem?' I said I hadn't a clue, whereupon Alastair said triumphantly, 'Eight minutes.' 'There you are. What more proof is needed. Leaderless groups are better than groups with a leader.'

Alastair looked somewhat deflated when I responded by saying that I did not think this proved that leaderless groups were better than groups with a leader. On the contrary, I told him that the game proved that each group needed a designated leader. In fact, there was a designated leader there all the time. 'How come?', asked Alastair. 'Do you mean that each group automatically selects a natural leader who emerges quietly, and in fact directs operations in the groups?' I replied that this was not the case, but that there was a quite unambiguous designated leader whom Alastair had failed to recognize. This leader was himself. He, Alastair, was carrying out the functions of high-level coordination, people development, process champion and management of change. First he had coordinated the training session, he had selected the leaders, he had spelt out the rules of the game, he had varied the rules for the sake of the experiment, and so on and so on. He had also carried out the people development functions of leadership. The exercise itself was designed to educate and train those involved. Alastair was trying to ensure good motivation, good fun and a climate in which learning could take place. If anyone had personal difficulties Alastair was there to sort them out. Likewise Alastair was accountable for carrying out, and improving, the course processes. He had devised the course curriculum and was accountable for the standards of quality and performance. The so-called 'leaders' Alastair had selected for the game were not really leaders at all, but unnecessary 'supernumeraries' whose roles were ill-defined and who, in truth, were getting in the way of the project by acting as a completely unnecessary filter for information and communication.

During my career as a management consultant, I have on many occasions advised clients to incorporate leaders with the four non-delegatable functions into their organizations. Many job descriptions have been prepared, training courses designed and assessment procedures developed around these functions. The effects have been striking with much greater clarity of role and a greater legitimization of authority resulting.

Competence in the non-delegatable functions has also been used as the basis for the selection of leaders. In contrast to many secular theories about leadership style – for example that good leaders must be uniformly participative rather than autocratic – the theologically derived roles demand a diversity of attributes. Good leaders need a blend of skills ranging from directive to consultative depending on the function being exercised.

CHAPTER 13

Participation

Finally the church is said to be 'mystical'. Many people think that the word 'mystical' means being transported out of one's normal mind into a dream-like state of higher consciousness. But this is not what the framers of the phrase 'mystical body of Christ' meant. They meant that the church is, in principle, a body of people totally united with one another through the mysterious inspiration of the Holy Spirit. Paul explains what 'being united' entails:

> Be completely humble and gentle; be patient, bearing with one another in love. Make every effort to keep the unity of the Spirit through the bond of peace. There is one body and one Spirit – just as you were called to one hope when you were called – one Lord, one faith, one baptism; one God and Father of all, who is over all and through all and in all.
>
> *Ephesians 4:2–6 (NIV)*

I must admit that for many years these verses were almost entirely unintelligible to me. To experience total unity with other people was light years away from my own experience. I was much more familiar with the feeling of not being in unity, of being an outsider, of being forced into a competitive mode of behaviour. Throughout my life I had been tempted to regard my fellow human beings with a certain wariness – from the war during my childhood, to the individualist and ambitious ethos that drove management to climb over each other in British Steel, to Mrs Thatcher's 'everyone for themselves' culture of the 1980s. But here, in stark contrast, was Paul talking of being of one mind, one body and one Spirit; echoing moreover Jesus' last prayer 'that all of them may be one, Father, just as you are in me and I am in you'.

My experiences with the Focolare had already helped me a great deal to understand what unity really entailed. In the company of the Focolarini I felt a deep divine unity. I know I experienced the nearness of God, the most intense joy, clarity of mind, an amazing sense of love for others, an inner courage in which I was ready to lay down my life for others, and a keen sense of moral discernment that wanted the best for others and didn't brook hypocrisy. Of course these feelings didn't last outside that circle of dedicated Christians. Normal life went on, often racked with sadness and inner tears, negative feelings and sinfulness. But having experienced the unity of 'Jesus in the midst' I knew it was far more real than the disunity of the world outside. Nothing could take that certainty away from me.

My impressions of the behaviour of workgroups on the other hand were of the 'worldly' variety. They did not experience the unity of Jesus at all. How could they? How could the average person doing his or her daily work possibly be expected to experience the intense joy inspired by the Holy Spirit? The 'real' world was not like that. I had been with dozens of workgroups, some reasonably happy and cohesive and others unhappy and divided, some friendly and others treacherous, but none united in the Spirit. The question I was asking myself was how could the behaviour of the average workgroup possibly be moved to resemble that of the ideal?

There is an old Chinese proverb which says, 'If you want to march a thousand miles you have to take the first step.' To turn workgroups into temples of the Holy Spirit was clearly a thousand-mile journey, so what was the first step?

There was one obvious way in which workgroups could be made more cohesive. I had frequently encountered workgroups simply physically unable to function as a closely-knit team because management had inadvertently put structural barriers in the way to prevent them. One typical barrier is to organize work-times of individuals such that the whole group is never at work at the same time. I have seen groups in which some people work from 6 a.m. to 2 p.m. and others from 8.30 a.m. to 4.30 p.m., and yet others on part-time contracts from 12 noon to 4 p.m., although they are all supposed to be collaborating in the same 'whole' task. Badly designed shift rotas produce the same results. It's as if during a church service people pop in and out when it suits them. Another divisive policy is to put people in the same workgroup on different conditions of employment from each other, for example blue collar and white collar. The problems this creates are compounded when the payment systems also differ between group members. Many companies have adopted 'individual pay for performance' systems, which explicitly promote competition and rivalry between members of the same team. All-round team performance is not rewarded.

I recall one bizarre incident when a works director boasted of the flexibility that existed between his shift operators while at the same time he was giving large bonuses to individuals he thought performed well.

The director offered to let me see for myself and took me to visit the control room in one of his big chemical plants. He called the shift team together (there were five of them) and introduced me. He then gave a lecture to all of us about the importance of working as a team, illustrating how everyone should help each other, be flexible and share each other's work, and so on. Then he turned to one of the team and said suddenly, 'What do you think of the bonus I've just given you?' The operator looked somewhat perplexed, so the director went on, half looking at me. 'Yes, I gave it to you because you are a hard worker and always pull your weight.' I could see a tinge of embarrassment come into the operator's face, and a rather more marked wave of resentment clouding the rest of the shift team. 'Come on, lad, don't be shy to speak,' said the director. After a pregnant pause, the operator let fly. 'I think it is the stupidest scheme I have ever come across,' he snapped. 'To tell you the truth, I feel ashamed to receive the money.' He then turned on the director. 'Do you know why you gave the money to me? I'll tell you why. It's because I speak up for myself more than the other men, because you notice me. But you haven't a clue what really goes on here. You don't know who does the real work and who keeps this place going when there is a problem here, do you?' The director stared into space. 'I'll tell you', the operator went on, 'who does the real work around here. It's Bob here.' With that, he swivelled round and pointed a finger to a little inconspicuous person standing in the shadows at the back of the group. 'That's Bob! Why didn't you give him the bonus? Or better still, if you really believe in teamworking for our shift, why don't you give us all a bonus?' The director thanked him for giving his point of view and we left. On the way back to his office he tried to persuade me that the reason for the operator's opposition was that he hadn't yet got used to the bonus scheme as it was relatively new, but he was sure the man would come to see sense sooner or later. 'After all,' he said, 'it works for me.' I didn't have the courage to argue with him.

There are several other ways in which it is possible to invent rules and procedures which positively prevent groups from functioning cohesively together – narrow job descriptions, poor layouts, trade-union-inspired demarcation and matrix structures are just some. These structural inhibitors must clearly be removed if workgroup members are to collaborate fully as a team. This is the first step in the thousand-mile journey. But it is only a first step, and basically it consists of simply removing constraints, or in other words creating equal opportunities for group members. Such changes on their own, however, do little to help the group become a team. Teamworking, in which people communicate fully with one another and help each other, requires a change of inner personal behaviour as well as of external, impersonal structures. I still needed to discover how this could be brought about.

CHAPTER 14

The Church's Indifference

Despite gratifying success in the field, few Christian people outside industry took the theological implications of my work seriously during the 1970s, the 1980s and the first half of the 1990s. I felt particularly acutely the indifference of the Church of England. There was very little interest in a theology of work based on the Holy Trinity. Indeed, most people – clergy as well as lay – seemed to be lamentably ignorant of any theology of the Holy Trinity; it tended to be regarded as a curious medieval relic from which the Reformation had liberated them. A few specialist theologians were the exception, but they seldom expressed any views about the world of work, nor related their theology to the great social and economic issues of today.

Ignorance and indifference to a theology of work was endemic at all levels within the church. Our former local parish priest was a fine man, meticulous in his pastoral concern for his parishioners. He was excellent at visiting the sick, arranging flower festivals, organizing carol concerts and collecting money to repair the church roof, but was reticent to explain how his Christian faith related to the major industrial, economic and social issues affecting the peoples of the world.

I found little more theological comprehension in that part of the church specializing in industry and work. Through the Industrial Committee, I had developed contacts with many industrial chaplains, whose pastoral duties related specifically to the industrial predicament. I once organized a series of two-day seminars for industrial chaplains: about 100 out of the then UK total of some 400 attended. I met many dedicated, good people and our discussions concerning a theology of work generated a temporary flurry of interest and illumination. But this quickly passed away and the chaplains returned to their normal ministries.

I also tried hard to interest the Industrial Committee itself, but for many years it was dominated by the Bishop of Middleton, Ted Wickham, whose overriding belief was that Christians should support economic growth at all costs. Other members, though individually distinguished, were collectively unable to agree on anything beyond harmless platitudes. Theology was seldom mentioned; few members wanted to discuss it. I once produced a ninety-page report on a theology of work, with which nobody agreed or disagreed, and which was then quietly discarded.

Occasionally, the higher echelons of the official church became briefly conscious of questions of industry and work, but with little effect. An example was when the then Archbishop of Canterbury, Dr Coggan, launched a 'Call to the Nation', inviting all people to reflect on and address the key economic and social issues facing them. Work-related issues came top of the list! As a result Dr Coggan decided to hold a consultation with three 'experts' in the study of work, and invited Harold Bridger (a founding member of the Tavistock Institute), Arthur Johnstone (head of Organization and Development at ICI) and myself to Lambeth Palace for a private meeting. We were each given five minutes to say our piece, after which there was a general discussion for forty-five minutes. This inordinately short time given to address some of the crucial issues of modern society illustrated nicely the priority the church gives to such issues, and it was not surprising that the Archbishop appeared to understand very little of what any of us were trying to say. I left feeling that the meeting had been a waste of time. However, it was agreed that Arthur Johnstone and I would hold a seminar for senior clergy on the subject of work and theology. The Archbishop promised to get in touch again when arrangements had been made by his office.

After three months, during which nothing happened, I was told that there was a problem: namely that technically the Archbishop had no executive authority in the Church of England. Only bishops had the authority to fund a seminar. Consequently a national seminar was almost impossible to arrange. However, there was a way round the problem since as Archbishop of Canterbury, Dr Coggan was also the Bishop of the diocese of Canterbury, and therefore could fund a seminar provided invitees came from the diocese alone. With a tinge of disappointment we agreed to the reduced scope of what I firmly believed was an issue of national importance.

Three more months passed. Then I was told that there was another technical hitch. The Board for Social Responsibility of the diocese of Canterbury had merged with the Board for Social Responsibility of the adjacent diocese of Rochester, so the seminar could not go ahead without formal agreement of both parties. After several more months we eventually held the seminar. Regretfully neither the Archbishop of Canterbury nor the Bishop of Rochester turned up; participants consisted of a few rural parish priests and some agnostic industrial chaplains. The 'Call to the Nation' had faded away.

I once heard a story which gives a possible explanation for the massive indifference to a trinitarian theology of work which seems to afflict so many Christians. It told of three people travelling in a wild country. One day they saw a strange parchment on the ground. The first person was a chemist who analysed the complex series of chemicals used in the production of the parchment, and he marvelled at the ingenuity of a primitive people. The second person was an artist who wondered greatly at the remarkable aesthetic sensitivity of a primitive people and their subtle use of colour, light and shade. The third person knew the language of the primitive people and read the message on the parchment, which warned intruders of the penalty of death if they trespassed on the people's territory. He ran away and the chemist and the artist were duly killed. They were looking in the wrong place for the meaning that mattered. Their skills were misplaced. In fact one could say that the greater their dedication as chemists and artists, the less likely they would be to think of reading the message.

It could be that the apparent incomprehension of the relation between God as trinity and work by many in the church is for similar reasons. The majority of church members in England today appear to be listening to a different language. For them theology is either a dead subject, and their Christian faith lies in worshipping, saying prayers and leading lives of personal love and uprightness, or theology is a means of understanding God more fully. The doctrine of the Holy Trinity is being used to give those people who are interested a closer glimpse of the inner nature of God. But I was on a different wavelength altogether. For me the Trinity is neither dead nor is it a vehicle for understanding God better. For me the doctrine of the Holy Trinity is the vehicle for understanding the world: not God out there; but our own world, in the here and now. In particular I had little doubt in my mind that the more nearly the structure of human work mirrored the 'structure' of God, the more wholesome, efficacious and satisfying it became.

In contrast to the indifference of the official church, there has been a growing interest in the subject of 'whole' work within secular circles. The concept of the 'basic transformation' to identify the key conversion features of work processes has been widely accepted. So has the notion of the 'whole' task. People regard it as simple common sense to organize each 'whole' task so that it can be operated by a small workgroup under a leader, whose members do 'whole' jobs and who are able fully to work as a cohesive team, and participate in each other's work.

I have also found warm support for including in the

'whole' task (the 'do') an originating component (plan) and an expressive component (evaluate). It is well understood that together these functions make work more 'whole'. In practice, this 'matching' process has also determined how to design work layouts and technology.

In the face of this level of secular appreciation, it was painful that the Church of England seemed so unwilling or unable to assimilate and proclaim the reality of 'whole' work. Deep in my soul I was troubled by the lack of support. The church after all was Christ's creation – his own bride. So why was there a blockage? Did the problem perhaps lie in the unique history and doctrinal ambivalence of the Church of England? Had the fact that it had been subordinated to the State by King Henry VIII fatally compromised it? Or did the problem lie in me and in my ideas? Was I down the wrong track, stretching analogies too far or looking for correspondences between theology and work which weren't really there?

Looking back to those days, I have come to the conclusion that neither explanation is satisfactory. I think that the real failure to communicate Christian realities lies in our own egoism and in the paucity of our inner spiritual lives. In my case I was too full of my own ideas and was blind to that wonderful eucharistic prayer, 'Lord I am not worthy to receive you, but only say the word and my soul shall be healed.'

CHAPTER 15

The Work-structuring Principles

When I was younger my father once said to me that however good one's ideas, they are no use to anyone unless they can be so expressed that they stimulate and inspire others to act. I would have saved a lot of time and energy had I listened to his advice. For he was not only an outstanding thinker but also a brilliant communicator. His seminal book *Small is Beautiful* (note the communicative power of the title) is full of memorable phrases which speak directly to the heart of the reader and have the power to change his or her life. I once asked him how he came by such pithy aphorisms. His answer was unexpected. He said 'I spend hours, days, mulling over what I am trying to say and how to express it compellingly. It doesn't happen easily. I work and work and work until I am satisfied'. The message struck home. If I wanted to communicate basic theological ideas to a Western industrial audience who were almost totally ignorant of theology, I would have to work very hard to find a persuasive language.

The challenge was how to translate the insights concerning the Holy Trinity and the church into a language which the industrial and commercial world could use as a basis for restructuring itself holistically. I therefore set to work to try to crystallize the theological insights into a simple and accessible set of principles relevant to the world of work. These have since come to be known as the seven work-structuring principles, which ever since their formulation have been the basis for all my practical work.

The seven principles and their connection with their theological roots are as follows:

1. In order to create the conditions in which human beings can reflect the work of God the Father as 'ultimate origin' of human work, work must be organized so that each workgroup and their leader can plan and organize as much of their own work as possible.

2. To allow the work of the Son to be manifest as the measure of 'whole' work, especially as it relates to his crucifixion and resurrection, the corresponding principle of work organization must ensure that work is organized around the basic transformations in the process to form 'whole' tasks.

3. To facilitate the work of the Holy Spirit as the power which directs, guides and communicates the skills, knowledge and motivation of the workgroup necessary to bring the work forward to its fitting end, the corresponding principle of work organization should be that each workgroup has the opportunity fully to evaluate its performance against agreed standards of excellence.

4. To encourage workgroups to participate, as far as possible, in the mystical nature of the church, the principle of work organization is that personal and structural conditions that encourage teamworking and participation in the wider organization should be established.

5. To build up the notion of workgroup as a body, with its emphasis upon the complementary and meaningful roles of its several members, the principle of work organization urges that jobs should be designed so that each workgroup member can personally plan, do and evaluate at least one transformation in the process.

6. To establish the corresponding need for leadership in a workgroup as exists in the church, where it is described as 'of Christ', the principle of work organization requires that each workgroup should include a designated leader.

7. To ensure that the workgroup size is within the range in which group members can communicate fully to one another, the principle of work organization is that the basic organizational unit should be the primary workgroup (in other words, four to twenty people).

It should be said straight away that I am well aware that these seven principles don't do justice to the magnificent and transcendent reality of the Holy Trinity or the church. The powers in God are infinitely greater than those directed at the world of work.

In any case, I regard the seven principles as provisional.

I would be only too pleased if a new wording could be found which communicates better the underlying theological realities, so that they breathe life and light into the hearts and minds of those who are striving for a reordering of the world of work.

On the other hand, the work-structuring principles have already succeeded in stimulating interest and enthusiasm from many people in industry who know nothing at all about theology. People have often said: 'The principles ring bells with me'; 'One cannot fault the logic'; 'They present in a systematic way what I have always believed'; 'I like the values behind the principles.' Also, the principles are all actionable and indeed have already led to action on a large scale. They have already borne much fruit. When they have been properly understood they have proved that they offer an effective framework for restoring the wholeness of work.

The principles are most powerful when they are accepted and implemented as an integrated set. Just as it is foolish to pick and choose significant parts of the Christian faith and reject others, so one cannot sensibly be selective about principles derived from that faith. It's all or nothing. The principles are interrelated; they support each other; they enhance each other; they draw meaning from one another; and they can't be implemented properly without each other. Their unity draws from the unity of faith, which ultimate derives from the primordial unity within God.

When the principles are applied together in practice, lasting benefits are obtained. Organizations have experienced major improvements in costs, product quality and yields, delivery times, work in progress, reliability, service and overall efficiency. At the same time there has also been increased job satisfaction, motivation and opportunity for self-development among working people. Sickness and absenteeism have fallen, safety standards have risen and workers have adopted a more responsible attitude to each other and to the wider community. The human benefits are particularly important since they are the well-springs of future improvements in creativity and efficiency. They are also motivational.

Many psychologists have studied motivation and have produced their own theories to explain it. A giant among the pioneers of psychoanalysis, Sigmund Freud, came to the view that the need for creativity was the prime determinant of motivation. His pupil, Adler, put more emphasis on the desire for power. Other psychologists give most weight to achievement (McLelland) and social relationships (Morris *et al.*). Hertzberg, who was mentioned in Chapter 5, believed that motivation was caused by a mix of factors which worked in combination with each other.

One of the remarkable things about the seven principles of 'whole' work is that each separate principle highlights a cause of motivation corresponding closely to one of those established by the empirical observations of these leading psychologists. Once again theology and science are in harmony. For example, the principle reflecting the work of God the Father emphasizes the power to originate, the freedom to determine what is to be done, the ability to plan and organize one's own work. This need for power was precisely the conclusion of Adler. Allegiance to a small group gives the opportunity for social relations, friendship and recognition, all of which again are motivators, as recognized by Morris and others. Again, the principle of feedback and evaluation is motivating, since it allows standards to be set and achievements to be measured against these standards (compare McLelland). The need for leadership is motivating in that we all have need for dependency, discipline and help in order to grow. Also, the principle defining a 'whole' job, which stems from the theological description of the church as a body, emphasizes the possibility of creative work as espoused by Freud. The principle that each workgroup should carry out the cluster of activities surrounding the basic transformation to form a 'whole' task, gives the work significance, variety and completeness, which in themselves are motivating. Finally, the teamworking principle offers opportunity for participation in the group's 'whole' task and is motivating for those who value teamwork, a need to belong, and who seek a deeper unity with other people. When all the principles are applied together, the opportunity exists for a whole range of motivating experiences from which individuals can draw according to their preferences.

I have been careful to say that each principle 'gives the opportunity for' different motivations, and not that it directly motivates. Note the words 'gives the opportunity for'. Structural principles merely provide a working environment conducive to motivation. For example, to place people in small groups merely ensures that group members can communicate with each other, be friendly towards each other and help each other. This does not mean that they will behave like that. As has been said, 'You can take a horse to water but you cannot make it drink.' On the other hand, work that is not structured according to theological principles actively prevents people from benefiting from the motivating potential of their work environment. If, instead of working as a small group, people have to work in long straight rows separated by several metres from one another, it is clearly physically impossible for them personally to communicate and help one another, even if they wanted to. It is the same with the other principles. Their presence gives the opportunity for better motivation, while their absence virtually effectively prevents these motivators from functioning at all.

In other words, unless work is organized on the basis of the theologically derived principles, the restoration of 'whole work' cannot even begin. They are the bedrock for rebuilding our industrial structures. Each principle not only reflects a basic theological and human reality, but all of them taken together constitute a powerful platform which is immeasurably greater than the sum of the parts.

CHAPTER 16

A Theology of Work in Practice

In 1981 I left the LSE and became a full-time self-employed management consultant with the ambition to introduce 'work structuring' (the name which had been given to the principles and methodology) to whomever was prepared to try it out. The work progressed well and I soon found myself working in some major 'blue-chip' companies. By 1986 I had more work than I could cope with and a decision had to be made whether to continue alone (there were enticing reasons favouring this option) or to join together with others to expand the work further.

I have to admit that to work with others posed something of a psychological threat, especially the responsibility of having to be an employer, with a regular wage bill to pay out. There were practical reasons, too, which made it difficult to expand in the short term. I knew very few people who possessed the set of skills needed to reconcile theology with the management of change in industry and elsewhere. Those I did know (one or two colleagues working with me as internal facilitators in client companies) were already gainfully employed.

On the other hand, there were compelling attractions in favour of ending self-employment: the adventure of building a team – of achieving unity with others; the huge possibilities in pooling one's creativity; and, not least, a stirring of the conscience which was saying that I had no right not to share the insights which I had been given. So gradually, one by one, I was eventually able to persuade six good, experienced managers, whose values and beliefs were similar to my own, to join me in 'spreading the word'.

At first it wasn't easy to find work for everyone. There were not many organizations in the mid-1980s who were prepared to take such a fundamental look at their operations as was implied using the work structuring approach. Those who were brave enough were also reluctant to hire an 'unknown' consultancy and even lesser-known consultants. Whereas I personally had been fortunate in having already built up a good clientele, the others had not and initially I experienced serious problems of handing work over to them, and they suffered consequential financial hardship.

Gradually, however, as more organizations came to hear about the principles and methodologies, the work grew. The results were good. When properly applied, the work structuring philosophy was able to bring about many simultaneous improvements to the host organization. These were not only 'bottom-line' results such as costs, quality and work-in-progress savings, but also reliability, delivery improvements and better customer service. In addition, and this was the most exciting feature, by introducing the work structuring principles the human indicators of well-being improved as well. Safety, accident rates, absenteeism, job satisfaction, involvement in suggestions schemes and other forms of continuous improvement – all showed significant gains. Managers remarked on the new spirit of cooperation, dedication to high standards and a desire to improve which characterized the restructured organizations.

The work diversified both in terms of the industrial and other sectors covered and geographically. Although my background had been in the steel industry, we quickly found ourselves heavily involved in the electronics, chemical and petroleum industries, in pharmaceuticals, detergents, bottle extrusion manufacture, the pigments industry, in power stations, furniture, non-ferrous metals, glass, prefabricated aluminium frames, washing-machine manufacture, tobacco, tyres and others. Beginning in production – where products were made – we were soon asked to look at the structure of research and development functions, as well as sales and marketing. From this wider span emerged requests to advise on the structure of total businesses.

Interest has also grown in sectors of the economy outside industry. In 1988 we were invited to restructure our first acute hospital; and this soon led into requests to structure other parts of the health service, such as general practice and community care. The work also spread into the banking sector, and one international bank has redesigned the work in all its branches along the lines of the work structuring principles. A recent area to show interest has been central government, and to date we have trained around fifty internal consultants employed by the UK government to use the work structuring principles and methodology.

The work has also spread overseas. Agencies have been set up in South Africa and the USA, and other countries are following. In addition, significant projects have already been undertaken in Ireland, France, Germany, Belgium, Canada, Panama and Malaysia; and smaller projects in several other countries. One of the world's largest international oil companies has asked us to restructure all its chemical operations worldwide and a similarly huge producer of household goods wants the same done to its European operations.

To underpin the practical work, we have also set up an interdenominational Theology Panel, consisting of a number of lay people and clergy, in order to develop and deepen our understanding of the theological and spiritual roots of 'whole' work. One of its first projects was a study of how to organize a parish using the work structuring principles.

The work has been hugely stimulating, fulfilling and demanding.

We have been humbled and amazed at the wide interest shown in recreating 'whole' work. The work structuring principles and methodology, stemming as they do from theological insight, work. They appeal directly to reason and common sense, and they produce results. There is no need to make explicit their theological antecedents any more than a doctor has to go through the theory of penicillin to a patient infected with a disease-causing bacterium. It is enough to describe the principles, demonstrate the methodology, point to the results and outline the underlying values: the resonances with the divine give the inner ring of truth. There is no need to proselytize.

In our literature we state what we stand for in purely human terms:

1. Central to our philosophy is the primacy of the human being in matters of work organization. Subject to the realities of the market-place, we stand firm in the belief that people come first. Strategies, structures and systems exist for people, and not the other way around.

2. Work structuring seeks to improve work at the level of the total work system. Our approach is holistic, systemic and comprehensive. Our philosophy and methodology allow all the major component elements of a work system to be positively transformed at the same time to achieve competitive efficiency and high performance, personal development, satisfaction for those involved and lasting excellence with net benefits for the community and the environment. Our systems-level approach sets out systematically to streamline and revitalize the system as a whole, and thus make the whole system healthy.

3. The work structuring approach seeks to equip organizations to bring about and sustain improvements by themselves. Our aim is not to impose but to teach the host organization all the necessary methodologies to improve, to

help clients to create the right climate for change and to work together with them to envision and achieve in practice the desired improvements, from beginning to end. Moreover, work structuring seeks to position client organizations so that the impetus for ever-deepening improvement, once initiated, naturally and actively develops within a learning culture, thereby ensuring sustained benefits both for the organization itself and for the community in which it is located.

4. The work structuring principles and methodology have been designed to be simple to understand, easy to use and compelling. They are accessible to everyone and bring about radical change. They are concerned with fundamentals, not with cosmetic appearances.

One of the more important outcomes of our work has been the discovery that when people carry out 'whole work' they find themselves in an environment which encourages their further spiritual development. To reach a spiritual awakening many people first need to travel down a purely human path of self-discovery as they untangle themselves from the web of conflicting structures and systems in which they have become enmeshed. Only then do they have the psychological space to improve their relationships with one another. Once people are doing 'whole' work, slowly but surely their sensitivity towards others becomes awakened and the sense of moral responsibility for the welfare of others increases. And since the healing process affects all of us, it also extends beyond the individual into the fabric of social and economic life itself. 'Whole work', in other words, has the power to draw people beyond itself and further along the spiritual path.

At the beginning of this process, people tend mostly to perceive only the operational advantages of implementing the work structuring principles. They notice that work can be undertaken more efficiently and sensibly. At the same time job satisfaction increases, and the scene is set for the next stage during which relationships between people deepen and they grow as responsible citizens. Then their spiritual life can also deepen.

Those of us who are Christians have a special role to play in creating 'whole work'. Our faith gives us two strategic advantages which are not available to other people of goodwill. The first is the unique contribution which Christian theology can make.

Why theology is so important to the holistic structuring of work is because theology is the bridge between scripture and holistic human structures. Through theology, God's words in scripture are made accessible to the human intellect. God's words of personal love, uttered to save mankind, are translated into mental conceptual structures. An outstanding example is the concept of the Holy Trinity. The Trinity, defined as three persons sharing one nature – God as three in one – is not mentioned as such in scripture. Scripture simply records the premises upon which this theological definition is based, insisting both that there is only one God and yet speaking of God the Father, his Son Jesus Christ and the Holy Spirit. It is left to theology to explain in a logical way how these premises can be made compatible with human reason. Through theology, in other words, divine revelation is translated into mental structures which are the fruits of the human mind, but which at the same time are an accurate 'reflection' of their divine antecedents. Furthermore, on the basis of the dictum 'as above, so below', the theologically articulated 'structures' within the human mind can be translated into a model for all human structures – as this book has tried to show.

Theology is not only a bridge between God's personal words of love and human structures, but the power of theology is that it identifies precisely that network of special principles and precepts which together provide a holistic understanding of structure. The seven work structuring principles are not just any randomly selected collection. They are archetypal or 'cardinal' in that all other principles derive from them. Together they form a carefully balanced mutually reinforcing set which reflects God's unity in creation. Other principles do not have the same power. Without the unity and clarity of thought that theology brings, attempts to create holistic structures quickly degenerate into an unintelligible maze of ad hoc initiatives and theories which cannot secure radical change. Sooner or later the 'good pagan' loses his way. When Christ said 'I am the way, the truth and the life' he meant it literally.

The other unique advantage claimed by the Christian is access to the strength and grace of the Holy Spirit through Christ. This is essential if one is to persevere in the huge task of transforming work and society. As Paul says, 'The fruit of the Spirit is love, joy, peace, patience, kindness, gentleness and self-control' – precisely the qualities needed to facilitate lasting change.

We hardly need to be reminded of the necessity, therefore, to use all the means made available to us through the church, to deepen our relationship with God. How to do this is an intensely personal matter. I do not feel qualified to advise anyone since I have to confess I find it difficult enough myself. For example, I try to pray: to give thanks, and to ask that I may be given the grace to strive harder for the redemption of work and society in a way God wants me to. But I often forget to pray, although I know in my heart that without regular prayer my good intentions can easily become corrupted. One of the biggest temptations in reforming work is that one can easily forget what one is doing it for. Creating 'whole work' can bring considerable material prosperity and recognition for the change agent as well as be an instrument for the spiritual development of the client, and it is all too easy to be seduced by the earthly benefits. Personally, I find it easiest to put aside short periods for prayer, such as when I get up in the morning or go to bed at night, or when I have a few moments waiting in a queue, or travelling in a bus, etc. I trust that God is never too busy to listen!

I also find that attending Holy Communion is very helpful. The central theme of this book has been to stress the importance of restructuring work so that small groups can plan, do and evaluate a basic transformation in order that they can mirror the small groups of Christians meeting to witness the real presence of Christ in the mystery of the

Eucharist. How much more important is it to actively participate in the real thing!

Finally, the study of scripture is very important. Christians of all denominations are united in the view that the Bible is the source document of their faith and that God's word is to be found in it. A Christian who does not know his scripture is like a motorist who does not know the Highway Code!

Without scripture, moreover, it is impossible to obtain an understanding of Christian theology, essential for those whose vocation it is to help proactively in the redemption of modern industrial work. As has been argued throughout this book, an understanding of 'whole work' derives directly from theology and is not revealed in scripture *per se*, although, of course, theology is derived from scripture.

CHAPTER 17

Some Case Studies

The impact of the work structuring principles on, successively, efficiency, motivation and ethical behaviour can be illustrated by referring to actual case examples. The first, showing efficiency and motivational gains, is a simple tabulation of some of the results obtained from a chemicals factory which underwent a restructuring process. Many similar examples could be cited. In the first fifteen months after implementation the following improvements were recorded.

Operational	Start	After 15 months
Plant efficiency (%)	92.1	97.0
Contamination per grade change (parts per million)	1.1	0.1
Customer service (on time delivery) (%)	80	97
Output approved (kg/h)	780	975
Working capital (£ million)	7.0	3.5

Motivational	Start	After 15 months
Suggestions (per 100 people/year)	70	200
Safety audit error	45	3
All injury rate (pa)	9.5	5.0
Discretionary absence (%)	3.75	1.0

A second example comes from a different factory where an assessment was made of the benefits of a work structuring project involving the reorganization of some 500 people. A senior manager from within the company had been asked to give an appraisal of the changes for the company chiefs. Here is the conclusion of his report. He was asked: What was achieved?

The answer is a much improved working structure, which has developed into a product-focused organization, with responsibilities from incoming to outgoing lorry, and is dedicated to the needs of its customers.

The methodical procedure which arrived at this result established:

- improved production processes with reduced waste;
- workgroups of essentially appropriate size;
- the necessary support staff in close proximity, allowing the workgroups to plan and evaluate their own activities.

The inclusion of planning and evaluation activities humanized work. They returned it to a natural and whole activity.

The right conditions to empower the workgroups were therefore put in the right place. Some believe that the attainment of production targets required in subsequent stock reduction exercises could not have been achieved without the improved organization as precursor.

From management's point of view, the changes have been clearly beneficial.

Devolution of engineering and quality control to the workgroups has led to a better understanding and faster response to customer requirements, lower stocks, reduced documentation, and more effective management of change.

The establishment of a sharper role for the group leader has provided the authority required to get things done, and to widen the tasks of the team members. Aspects of quality control and process improvement have been undertaken by team members.

Numbers of the management and operatives have reduced. One level of management has been removed, creating a flatter organization. The immediacy of support staff and the capacity of the workgroup to undertake certain tasks themselves allowed net reductions in what had formerly been the central technical and quality control functions. Charting and streamlining of processes resulted in a reduction of the number of operatives required for materials handling, as well as coincidentally reducing 'in process' stocks.

Operatives are now members of smaller groups, and

therefore closer to their managers, but with reduced opportunity for job rotation.

They have been relieved of very physically demanding tasks, but asked to take on a number of former staff activities, including weight checks and certain analyses.

Full participation of the working groups now exists in:

- meeting quantity and quality targets
- wastage reduction
- maintenance
- health and safety
- training etc.

Those whose jobs have been enhanced say that their working life is more interesting. Others say that their purpose in coming to work is to earn money, and they are not particularly interested in what they do.

It is perhaps unreasonable to expect more in a time of recession, against a backcloth of reducing numbers. What is being looked at for now is stability and security. It is encouraging that despite the difficulties, constructive ideas for improvement are still being offered by the workforce.

The exercise provided an organization that was flat, lean in numbers and effective.

Today much is written of flow processes, elimination of waste, team working, empowerment of the workforce, flat organizational structures and so on. JIT ['just in time'] and TQM ['total quality management'] seek to eliminate production problems, focusing respectively on waste reduction and zero defects.

Schumacher's work structuring involves the workforce and humanizes work. It delivers the sought-after organization which provides an essential framework for all these initiatives.

Improvements such as these have occurred in many parts of the industrial sector, where work is particularly badly dehumanized. They are the start of the healing process. The beginning is modest, but the important point is that it triggers further efforts to stimulate teamwork and the development of deeper human relationships. These in turn encourage a greater sense of social and environmental responsibility. Ethical issues then enter the equation. The process of renewal is under way.

There have been similar opportunities – and an equally urgent need – to restore 'whole work' in almost every other sector of the economy, including the health and academic sectors. One would think, for example, that those who are professionally engaged in looking after the good health of other people would be able to keep their own organizational house in order. Not so. The deviation from holistic principles is just as great in the health service, from which a third case example has been drawn.

One day in March 1991, the telephone rang. It was a public health consultant from Cardiff in Wales. He had been given my name by a mutual colleague, and wanted to meet. I remember well that we met one evening in the Cwrt Bleddyn Hotel, outside Usk. I was engaged in restructuring a large industrial plant in Newport at the time, and used to spend the night at the hotel. The doctor asked about my consultancy work, and after I had described it to him, he said he very much liked the values underpinning it and would like to explore the possibility of some form of collaboration. He was part of a team determining the role of, and designing, a prototype 'neighbourhood hospital' in South Glamorgan, and felt that a work structuring input might be helpful. I readily agreed, and the good doctor set about persuading the local health authority and social service department to sponsor my involvement in the project.

In a very short time, the health authorities were persuaded to provide adequate funding and the work began. Our aim was to determine the role of the proposed hospital in the context of community care in the area, and then to create 'whole' work within it. We soon discovered that although the concept of the National Health Service is exemplary, in reality it suffers from the same deformation of work as does industry and commerce. Fragmentation of tasks, bureaucracy, narrow professional demarcations, selfish vested interests which put the patient last, are rampant. The excessive fragmentation of work is particularly damaging. For example an elderly infirm lady requiring care at home is washed and dressed by a district nurse, (or possibly by a local authority home carer or community care aide); she receives footcare from a chiropodist; her shopping and housework is done by a local authority home carer; meals are provided by the local authority meals-in-the-home department, or by the WRVS; her laundry is collected by the local authority laundry service; her house maintenance and repairs are carried out by the local authority housing department; the provision of a wheelchair, tripod or stick requires collaboration between the physiotherapy department of the local hospital and an occupational therapist; if she needed her lavatory seat raised, or a bath stool and stick, she would have to get permission from an occupational therapist; if she needed incontinence pads the district health authority district nurse would become involved; if she felt ill the local GP would have to come along, and if she needed financial or other benefits, the local authority welfare rights workers would deal with her problems. You can imagine the confusion and complexity existing in the various departments and sections engaged in providing what should be a seamless package of care to an old lady, and also the confusion and anxiety suffered by the lady, as one person after another marches up the garden path and knocks on her front door.

To find a way through this morass, we had to get back to basics. What were the basic transformations in the healing processes (in other words, the 'crucifixion – resurrection' processes), to be covered by the hospital? How should the resources needed to carry them out be organized? How could we build the trinitarian concept of 'plan, do, evaluate' into the structures? How could people sensibly be organized into small, cohesive groups? What implications did all this have on the scale, architectural design and layout of the hospital?

We started out by seeking to identify all the basic transformations in which the community health service is engaged. We provisionally found twelve. These were:

1. *Ill to well*

This transformation is the change from a state of ill health to an acceptable level of health.

2. *Carer stressed to carer unstressed*

This is usually described as respite care, where a chronically ill dependent patient is looked after for a period to give the carer a break. It is the carer who experiences the change from a damaging state of stress to an acceptable level.

3. *Terminal condition to death*

The hospice transformation – through the reduction of pain and discomfort, and by allowing those facing death to die with dignity.

4. *Pregnant to healthy mother and child*

The primary health care team's contribution to making the maternity process a safe one for mother and baby during pregnancy and early infancy.

5. *Psychologically distressed to relaxed*

The first stage is that of a person whose mental condition is such that he is disturbed, anxious or depressed. The causes may be endogenous or exogenous. for example unwanted pregnancies, job loss, deprivation, family breakdown.

6. *Unprotected to protected*

The immunization process.

7. *Dependent to independent (therapy)*

The person has lost his independence due to a severe physical problem (e.g. a stroke or loss of a limb) or a mental handicap (e.g. Downs syndrome). After an initial stable state has been reached, the transformation is the restoration of independence by the provision of a finite course of therapy.

8. *Dependent to independent (technical)*

Similar to 7, except that restoration to independence is dependent upon the provision of complex mechanical or electronic aids.

9. *Unsafe (curable) to safe*

The problem may be simple, e.g. a minor injury or complex, e.g. a person of limited mental capability with a fractured leg. In this latter case the transformation would be to cure the fracture, but the process may require the person to be looked after during the cure to prevent him injuring himself further.

10. *Unsafe (incurable) to safe*

The long-term care of the person to maintain his safety. The typical case would be an elderly mentally infirm patient. It implies maximizing independence and minimizing deterioration.

11. *Unhealthy behaviour to healthy behaviour*

This transformation embraces all forms of health promotion including the ability to cope and the adoption of healthy lifestyles.

12. *Dependent (unmaintained) to dependent (maintained)*

The transformation is to establish and continue the maintenance of a person, usually frail and elderly, who will always need maintenance. As for 10, it implies the promotion of the highest possible level of independence and minimizing deterioration.

Each of these transformation processes is made up of a series of interrelated activities (for example nursing, medical interventions, home care, etc.) which form a mutually dependent and causally related set. They are analogous to the 'total pattern of Christ's life'. Using the terminology described earlier, we could see that each of these individual transformations and their support activities formed a 'whole' – they comprised a 'whole' task.

As we have seen, a central tenet of a holistic approach to work design is that interconnected tasks ('whole' tasks) should be carried out by integrated groups of people under a common authority structure (reflecting the church as mystical body of Christ). In this way there is created a synergy between the operational interconnections inherent in the work process and the organizational interconnections found within managed groups of people. The organization is made to follow and match the process.

If resources were infinite, it could be argued that each separate transformation process should be carried out by a separate group of people with the specialist skills and time necessary to devote to that process. But resources are scarce, and in any case there are overlaps between several of the twelve processes identified above.

These were, in other words, subsets of more fundamental transformation processes. It was therefore necessary in practice to analyse the strength of linkage between the twelve transformations to determine whether they should be organized together or not. When this analysis had been carried out, we found that they grouped themselves into four more or less independent areas, each centred on a key basic transformation. These were:

(A) A cluster including the mentally distressed, hospice, independent (therapy) and safe (curable), all strongly linked to the ill–well transformation.

(B) A strongly tied cluster embracing maternity, health promotion and protection (for example immunization), with strong links to the general practitioner.

(C) A cluster consisting of respite care, unsafe (incurable)/safe and unmaintained/maintained dependent which centred around the care of the elderly.

(D) The dependent–independent (technical) transformation of the physically disabled.

Following the principles of 'whole' work, we concluded that separate organizations should be responsible for managing each cluster of interrelated transformations.

This analysis proved extremely interesting to the healthcare professionals. They discovered that this way of dividing the health services allowed their resources to be

173

clustered around clear and distinct health gain areas. Thus the ill/well cluster (cluster A) contained a series of activities which could combine nicely into the remit of a short-stay neighbourhood hospital, which was the subject of our consultancy brief. Cluster B on the other hand, could be neatly assimilated into the existing structure of general practices. Cluster C turned out to consist precisely of those interrelated activities which were needed to look after elderly infirm people, such as the lady in the example above. Under this concept all the mainline services needed to look after a person with multiple needs could be organized within the same integrated structure, thus providing a much more efficient and user-friendly service. Finally, cluster D was identified as a special need which was best provided for by a specialist agency unconnected with the other three main healing clusters.

Once the boundaries of the respective 'whole' tasks within the healing professions had been established, it was then possible to examine the practical mechanisms by which each 'whole' task could be planned, done and evaluated by manageable-sized groups of people. The introduction of these theological concepts made possible the greatest possible degree of self-responsibility and autonomy in each area as well as ensuring adequate feedback of quantifiable information to determine the performance of the various groupings. They also provided a context for the development of teamworking. Finally, they gave a set of parameters within which the new neighbourhood hospital could be designed in terms of such things as numbers of rooms, locations, facilities to be provided (including day care) and staffing.

I hope that these examples have given a flavour of the first steps in a process leading initially to greater efficiency, standards of service and job satisfaction, and then to the development of teamworking and improved personal relationships. However, as already mentioned, the journey does not end there. We are also drawn along a spiritual path, this time towards a growing sense of moral responsibility for others.

That participating in 'whole' work increases people's sense of moral responsibility is evident by the facts. I have witnessed the process many times. As an example I remember once restructuring part of a semiconductor factory. Performance and motivation improved significantly, in contrast to the rest of the factory which remained tense and inefficient.

The factory looked out over a large grassy area, which had been bought by the company in anticipation of a possible expansion. A number of rabbits and other small creatures had made their home there. One day the administration manager decided that the field needed 'tidying up', and so he gave an order to exterminate the rabbits and other animals. Significantly, the people in the restructured part of the factory objected strongly to the decision, and succeeded in having it reversed. Workers in the rest of the factory remained indifferent. What had happened was that those people carrying out 'whole' work had become more sensitive to ethical considerations. Those who were alienated from their work hadn't.

Later the rest of the factory was restructured and similar improvements occurred – but not quite the whole of the rest of the factory. There was one department which was top secret into which no one was allowed entry without special authorization. I learned that it was engaged in making components for nuclear warheads. The department badly needed restructuring and since I had by then been working in the factory for some years, and was trusted, I was one day asked by the works director if I would extend the work to that department. I declined. When asked why I said that every human being has to make his or her own decision as to what is morally right or wrong for them personally, and that for me I drew the line at making the nuclear armaments trade more effective. I said that this was my personal choice and that I had no desire to imply judgment of others who might feel differently. The works director said he was surprised but accepted my decision with understanding. I noticed, however, that he, and other managers, would raise the subject with me again from time to time. Eventually it emerged that they too were uneasy about the morality of what they were doing, but they had somehow been sucked into it by some corporate-level decisions made some years before.

One day the works director asked to see me and told me, beaming, that they had decided to discontinue their Ministry of Defence contract. 'When it came up for renewal, we put in an uncompetitive tender,' he said with a twinkle in his eye. 'We've worked out how to redeploy the workforce and in any case we want to develop some other more socially useful products.'

It is not always the case that the ethical dimension of an assignment is as simple to handle. Sometimes it is difficult to know where the ethical line should be drawn. On one occasion some years ago, I was asked to restructure a large tobacco factory in Bristol. Should I help an organization to improve itself when it was making what only some people (at that time) regarded as a harmful product but others did not? I consulted a good friend who was a priest. Should I take on the assignment or not? He gave me an excellent piece of advice. He said, 'If you are unsure, do it. But if you find out later that it was the wrong decision, stop immediately'. I took his advice, so began work and to my surprise I grew more and more to like the people working in the tobacco factory. They were innovative, open-minded, honest, good fun, hard-working and decent people. Many of them did not smoke. Yet they made 'fags'. It struck me as strange that such a good bunch of people could devote themselves so energetically to producing such a questionable product.

What was even stranger was that their situation contrasted markedly with another organization with which I was associated at the time. For several years I had served on the board of a national charity. Unlike the tobacco company, their purpose and objectives were irreproachable. They ran hostels for the homeless, drug addicts and alcoholics. They looked after single mothers and people below the poverty line. Yet unlike the people in the tobacco factory, they were too often narrow-minded, stubborn and unwilling to change. And many of them smoked! How odd it was! Perhaps the explanation for the paradox lies in the fact that we are all incurable mixtures of good and evil, although we manifest our darker sides in different ways; some in what we do, others in how we do it.

Anyway, I continued with the work structuring project in the tobacco factory which proceeded smoothly and imaginatively. Plans were laid down to re-layout the entire factory, to create small groups of people who could plan, do and evaluate 'whole' tasks, and participate more fully in the creative process. An ambitious scheme costing £2 million was put together, which had the enthusiastic support of everyone up to Board level. Board approval was guaranteed. Then, totally out of the blue, the day before the crucial Board meeting, the company was taken over, the Board was sacked and all investment projects (including mine) were stopped. I remembered the words of my friend the priest: 'Stop immediately'. I did, but not quite in the way I expected!

The story, however, did not end there. About three years later I received a telephone call at my office. A voice said 'You won't remember me, but my name is ——. I was the chief engineer at the tobacco factory where you once worked in Bristol. I have just resigned, and I am looking for a job. Can you help me? I said I would try, and made several enquiries among other companies I was working with, but to no avail. Two months later the phone rang again, and my friend the chief engineer said, 'I just wanted to thank you for trying to help, and to let you know that you don't need to worry any more, because I have found a new job near my home with a small engineering company.' I congratulated him, and just before putting the phone down, was prompted to ask what, if anything, had happened to the work structuring programme after I had left the factory three years before. He told me with some emotion that the management team were bitterly disappointed that the project had been cancelled, so much so that they decided to go ahead anyway (unofficially) within a part of the factory, using funds cobbled together from various maintenance and other budgets. The results, he said, were outstanding. The people involved had benefited through acquiring increased skills, through growing self-confidence and better relations with one another. Performance, too, was better: less waste, fewer breakdowns, less hassle and so on. My friend said that it was the best thing he had ever done in his working life, and he was determined, if he did nothing else, to carry out the same programme to empower the people in his new engineering company. I was delighted at this further evidence that what was good about my work had remained intact and had been transferred elsewhere. My satisfaction was nearly complete when I learned later that the tobacco factory had closed down. I would have been totally satisfied if those people who had acquired greater skills and self-confidence through their work had found other jobs without difficulty, as a result. Perhaps they did. I firmly believe that good processes eventually lead to good outcomes.

CHAPTER 18

The Creed

It is not without significance, indeed it is immensely significant, that the principles of 'whole' work in their theological form are echoed in the main parts of the Christian Creed itself – the bedrock of the Christian faith. Such a correspondence is another confirmation of the real nature of the parallels between good human structures and relationships and revealed 'divine' structures and relationships. The Creed says:

I believe in one God, the Father almighty, maker of heaven and earth, and of all things visible and invisible:
  And in one Lord Jesus Christ, the only-begotten Son of God, begotten of his Father before all worlds, God of God, Light of Light, very God of very God, begotten, not made, being of one substance with the Father, by whom all things were made; who for us men and for our salvation came down from heaven, and was incarnate by the Holy Ghost of the Virgin Mary, and was made man, and was crucified also for us under Pontius Pilate. He suffered and was buried, and the

third day he rose again according to the scriptures, and ascended into heaven, and sitteth on the right hand of the Father. And he shall come again with glory to judge both the quick and the dead: whose kingdom shall have no end.

And I believe in the Holy Ghost, the Lord, the giver of life, who proceedeth from the Father and the Son, who with the Father and the Son together is worshipped and glorified, who spake by the prophets. And I believe one holy catholic and apostolic Church. I acknowledge one baptism for the remission of sins. And I look for the resurrection of the dead, and the life of the world to come.

Here, in consummate brevity, lies the essence of all the key ideas which provide the link between God and his creation. The Creed first refers to God the Father, the ultimate source of all creation, maker of heaven and earth, the origin of all that is, the great 'Planner' of the universe. Then it talks of God the Son, begotten of his Father, by whom all things were made, the great 'Doer' who was transformed from death to life – the archetypal transformation process which all creation must follow. Third, it acknowledges the Holy Spirit, the Lord and giver of life, who inspires, helps and leads all things towards the Spirit of truth, unity and goodness by freely convincing them of their value and worth. All three persons together are co-equal: they plan, do and bestow value (e-value-ate). Then the Creed continues, 'I believe in one church'. It thus acknowledges the mystical body of Christ, the eternal exemplar for all groups of people, including those at work. And finally, when the Holy Trinity and the church are established on earth in their perfection, the Creed concludes with its awesome hymn of hope. 'I look for the resurrection of the dead, and the life of the world to come'. The world, including that of work, will be divinely transformed.

It was thrilling to uncover the relationship of human work to the Creed. In the past I had often wondered what the relevance of the Creed was to loving God or one's neighbour. The Creed was not to be found in scripture. Yet every Sunday we were made to recite it in church. Surely the Beatitudes or some other summary of Christ's teaching would have been a much better agenda for personal Christian action!

I now realized that the Creed has nothing directly to do with living a better personal Christian life. It is not written in the language of divine love as found in the Gospels. Nor is it much use as a guide to moral behaviour. To look to it for moral guidance is as futile as to study chemistry in order to be able to read. The Creed is an archetypal conceptual structure, an organization of ideas and mental constructs whose function is quite different. The great power of the Creed is that it is a template for action in the world, in the realm of structures and organization. Moreover the theological principles summarized in the Creed are not only relevant to structures as they manifest themselves in the world of work, but to all structures and systems throughout the whole gamut of life: in science, medicine, politics, economics, sociology, psychology and any other discipline one cares to mention. In fact the only reason why the seven principles can restore 'whole' work is that the same principles are the precondition for the healthy development of any 'system' or 'being'. The Creed proclaims the 'structure' of God and his church in order that the world may be structured in that image and likeness. The Creed is thus the archetype for holistic economic, social and all other human structures. It is the map through which the modern industrial world can find its way out of the terrible entanglement in which it is becoming ever more deeply lost. The reason why the early church proclaimed God as a Holy Trinity was not in order to satisfy a meddling human curiosity about his inner nature. God revealed himself as trinity to save the world, his world. Also he didn't give us his mystical body the church to be some sort of club to which a dwindling minority of the population go on Sundays; he founded it because it offers to the whole human race the guiding principles for all forms of collective relationship and human development. When all the theological principles are fully present, and in proper proportion to one another, all living beings display the signs of wholeness or health. When any one of them is deficient, the being's inner structure – its immune system – no longer functions properly.

To understand this better the theological principles need to be lifted out of their work-related context and re-expressed as universal propositions.

1. The first principle expresses the originating freedom of God the Father and is thus concerned with the independence and self-sufficiency of the parts and the

whole of any created being or system. This may be called the principle of Autonomy.

2. The second principle expresses the activity of God the Son in creation and is thus concerned with the dynamic expression or issuing forth of the related activities which gives the being its unique nature, identity and purpose. This may be termed the principle of Transformation.

3. The third principle expresses the activity of the Holy Spirit and is thus concerned with the mechanisms by which the being undergoes self-evaluation and relates to the wider world.

These complex functions may be summarized by the term Evaluation.

4. The fourth principle derives from the church as mystical and thus concerns the degree of cohesiveness or 'fit' of the being's parts with each other and with the whole. This may be interpreted as the principle of Integration.

5. The fifth principle derives from the church as body and thus expresses the extent of internal distinctiveness of function or elements within the being. It may be known as the principle of Differentiation.

6. The sixth principle relates to the church as being 'of Christ' and thus points to the mechanisms through which the parts are coordinated in a purposeful harmony. This may be called the principle of Authority.

7. Finally, the seventh principle recognizes that creation itself needs to be properly proportioned, and so there is a need to determine the optimum material size or scale of the being or structure under consideration. This may be termed the principle of Right Scale.

CHAPTER 19

Systems and Components

In the biological and social sciences living beings are often referred to as 'sentient systems'. A human being or an animal or a plant is such a system because all its parts are interconnected, act and react on each other and on their environment, and all collaborate to achieve a common goal or purpose. When a number of sentient systems are put together the result is a 'social system'.

Social systems may be contrasted with 'technical systems', such as a machine which also consists of a number of complementary mechanical parts, working together to achieve a common result.

A work organization is also a 'system' because it consists of many functions acting together to achieve a common end. It may be termed a 'socio-technical system' insofar as it consists of human beings and technology together.

A useful distinction may be made between a 'systems-level' problem and a 'component-level' problem. Take a motor car, for example. The car, and its driver, may be termed 'a system'. It consists of a number of parts, some technical, some biological, which interact with each other, and which work together, hopefully harmoniously, to produce an outcome – in this case driving from A to B. One car and driver (one system) is easily distinguished from another car and driver (another system).

A component-level problem occurs when a component of the car goes wrong, say there is a flat tyre. To solve this problem one first has to identify it, then isolate it (by taking the wheel off), and then remedy it (by putting on the spare tyre). With luck the car is then in exactly the same state as it was before the problem arose, and one can drive off happily.

Now let us imagine that for some reason one drives off without repairing the tyre. What happens is that the car bumps around on the flat tyre; eventually the wheel buckles; the axle twists; soon the crankshaft goes out of alignment; one can't steer the car any more and one hits a tree with a nasty bump.

The problem, which started out as a component-level problem, has now affected the entire system. The effects of the flat tyre have spread out to infect the whole car. The problem has now become a systems-level problem which can no longer be solved by replacing the tyre, nor probably by replacing any other component. The whole system is damaged. The car is a write-off! Possibly the driver also!

To give another example, Diana and I have a friend who used to work in the Department of the Environment dealing with water research in the UK. He told us that in the past, when there were impurities or harmful bacteria in the water, the water boards used to identify them, isolate them and then remedy the situation by putting some antidote in the water to neutralize their effects, often a chlorine compound. The water could then be drunk as before. Putting in the chlorine was a component-level solution like replacing a tyre.

However, water pollution continues to grow at an alarming rate. The Department of the Environment is getting extremely worried because there are now so many chemicals in the water that they are setting up their own chain reactions producing new chemicals which, when combined with the old, have no known predictability. The problem has become a systems-level problem, since chemical cause-and-effect chains are spreading new forms of pollution throughout the water spontaneously.

The significance of this change in the nature of the problem is that it demonstrates that it is no longer possible to remedy water pollution by putting in yet other chemicals to neutralize the ones in there already. Or, making a general point, one cannot rectify systems-level deficiencies by using component-level solutions. In fact they may even make matters worse. Systems-level problems can only be solved by using systems-level solutions.

Unfortunately, for the last 300 years or so we, in the industrial countries, have been brought up to believe that we could solve most of our problems using component-level methodologies. In particular we have been using what is known as the scientific method. The scientific method works by firstly identifying a problem, then isolating it, then remedying it by finding a means of neutralizing its effects, usually by using laboratory controlled experiments. This is classic component-level methodology. It predominates in most disciplines. In medicine, for example, the offending bacterium is identified, isolated and remedied with the application of a specific drug which kills the bug while leaving the rest of the human body more or less in the state it was in before the bug arrived.

Many of the really big and intractable issues of our age, however, are not component-level problems at all; indeed most of them have developed because of our inability to connect the components or parts to the whole. They are systems-level problems. The big diseases – cancer, coronaries, arthritis, AIDS, much mental illness – affect the human system as a whole. The big economic problems of our day – inflation, poverty, unemployment, resource depletion and pollution – affect the entire economic system; one can't intervene in one area without the repercussions being felt in other areas. Similarly with the big problems of the inner city, of education, of social deprivation and particularly, of course, of the environment, including transport, water and waste. They are all systems-level problems and they can't be solved using component-level remedies such as the scientific method alone. There needs to be a change of perception and a recognition that these problems cannot be solved piecemeal without understanding their effect on the total system in which they are embedded. How, then, are systems-level problems to be solved?

To solve a systems-level problem one has to ask: what needs to be done to make the system as a whole flourish? What are the irreducible primary conditions for total social, economic or medical health? To find this out, one has to go back to first principles, back to basics. But what is 'basic'? Ultimately, existence itself could be said to be the most basic stuff from which all tangible things derive. So the question becomes: what are the essential characteristics of any existing living being?

It does not take much imagination to realize that, if God is the creator, for all created living beings to be 'whole' or healthy they must bear the same structural characteristics as their divine exemplar. In other words they must conform to the theologically derived principles. As above so below.

Let me give two brief examples of the enormous potential for solving some of the most intractable systems-level problems of modern industrial society by using the theologically derived principles. The first example comes from the field of energy policy. One of my wife Diana's many interests is how to develop a sustainable, environmentally benign energy supply to safeguard the quality of life of our children and children's children. She has written a well-respected book on the subject entitled *Energy: Crisis or Opportunity*, and is often called upon to give talks and seminars on the subject.

The so-called 'energy problem' is, of course, another systems-level problem which cannot be solved by single component-level 'magic bullets', such as relying on the free market to determine supply, or even by the mandatory application of renewable resources. The problem is now of such a magnitude that it has become interrelated with the economic destiny of whole countries, linked with massive environmental threats and resource depletion issues. Like the problem of work itself, it can only be solved by adopting integrated, holistic systems-level solutions. Again the same seven theologically derived principles provide the key.

1. Autonomy. This principle, reflecting the work of God the Father, would seek to ensure that there is the maximum delegation of responsibility for energy policy to the grass-roots, or at least to the lowest practical decision-taking level. Decentralization to local government creates empowerment and an atmosphere of self-responsibility.

2. Transformation. God the Son incarnates the original vision of God the Father. The nature of an energy system is to transform stored into useful energy. This means that useful energy must be available to everyone, that the most favourable balance must be struck between energy inputs and total energy outputs through efficiency of conversion and maximum energy conservation.

3. Evaluation. The Holy Spirit inspires all things to reach their destined goal. In energy terms this requires that each community agrees levels and standards of responsible consumption and supply, and measures the quantity and quality of energy usage against them. For people to be responsible for their energy use they must have information about the effects this has on others and on the environment. Without information and evaluation, no learning and responsible action can take place.

4. Integration. This reflects the 'mystical' nature of any living system and stipulates that the various elements

comprising an energy policy should display a powerful degree of cohesiveness, both internally and in relation to the wider community of which it is a part. It follows that energy systems must also be designed in a modular configuration so that communities have the freedom to respond to changes in supply as and when they occur.

5. Differentiation. Reflecting the notion of 'body', energy systems should be diversified to provide the best 'fit' between available energy sources and the energy user. Energy consumption patterns vary in accordance with people's needs as do the types of available energy which would best supply those needs.

6. Authority. The church is 'of Christ' and implies right leadership. In energy terms this recognizes that energy policy in each community should be coordinated. But since there are limits to the capacity of each local community to achieve optimum use of energy without some collaboration and cooperation with regional and national bodies, some wider coordination is also needed.

7. Right Scale. This implies that energy supply systems should technically be designed to a 'human scale' – in other words, to serve local communities of an economically self-sustainable size. This principle reflects the finiteness of all things within the unity of creation.

Unfortunately, space does not permit a full analysis of these principles and their translation into specific energy policy measures. But it is easy to see that they provide a powerful template against which particular decisions may be made. Take nuclear energy for example. It is quite obvious that a nuclear-based energy policy is almost totally incompatible with nearly every theologically derived principle. It precludes local autonomy; it is immensely wasteful in terms of conversion efficiencies and conservation; it is shrouded in secrecy; the technology is not of a human scale; and it is not easily integrated into a policy of energy supply diversification. An energy policy based on the theologically derived principles, on the other hand, provides a valid basis for holistic structural reform and is wholly compatible with other human, economic, environmental and resource imperatives. Its validity derives from its faithfulness to the Creed and from the fact that it produces positive results. The principles address at the most fundamental level the problems of the energy system as a whole.

A second example of how the seven theologically derived principles can restore health to human structures and systems came to my notice during the restructuring of a major pharmaceutical company. Among the therapeutic areas which were being investigated by the company was the area of oncology. For years they had been in the forefront of research into a variety of drug-based interventions to ameliorate the effects of various forms of cancer. No cure has yet been found, despite the fact that millions of pounds have been spent looking for new drugs.

During the course of the work at the pharmaceutical company I began to wonder whether diseases like cancer (and other similar diseases which affected the body or the immune system as a whole) were systems-level diseases which could only be solved by systems-level solutions. If so, could one beneficially apply the theologically derived principles to that system to effect a cure?

I was under no illusions that this was a wildly speculative question, but as there were several medical experts in cancer at the company, I had the opportunity to investigate the approach with experienced scientists from the outset.

Since cancers are unwanted cellular growths, the first task was to establish at what level of detail in the human body the 'system' responsible for the growth of cells could be found. Should one be examining body–mind–spirit (the 'whole' person) or just the body, or a function of the body such as the liver or blood, or single cells, or parts of a cell, or what? I needed to find the lowest level at which all the characteristics of the relevant system were manifest. At too low a level of detail, the characteristics of the system governing cell reproduction would be lost. At too high a level the cause-and-effect chains stimulating growth would become too diluted.

I therefore enquired at which level in the human body's anatomical structure could be found the function which both had the characteristics of a system and was responsible primarily for controlling the reproduction of potentially cancer-forming cells. The answer which came from the experts was that there are several functions within the body which control cell reproduction, depending on which type of cell one is considering. But most commonly the organ associated with many cancers is the liver.

Having focused on the liver, the next step was to ask two

questions. First, what was the mechanism (chemical or other) which could enhance the function of the liver governed by each theological principle? For example, taking the principle of authority, was there a substance or chemical which controlled the functioning of the liver? The second question: if these chemicals or substances were no longer ensuring the full functioning of the liver, had medical science discovered a method of stimulating or restoring that aspect of the liver's operation?

I was fascinated to discover not only that each of the seven theologically derived principles described a different function, but that when these functions were deficient they could be stimulated or restored to health by a known intervention. For example, the principle of autonomy (expressing the originating freedom of God the Father) applies to the liver and each of its major parts. In normal states of health, each part enjoys an optimum degree of independence and self-sufficiency. When the liver can no longer operate autonomously, it is usually because an offending stimulus is preventing it. This is usually bacterial, viral or toxic.

By removing these inhibitors, the principle of autonomy can be restored. Even more fascinating was the fact that some functions could be restored by using certain drugs, while others required a change in lifestyle or behaviour (such as diet, exercise) to make them perform properly.

If it is true that many cancers are systems-level diseases which cannot be cured by 'component-level' interventions, but can be resolved through the full application of the theologically derived principles, then it is clear that many of the ingredients for its cure are already in existence. What is required is a balanced cocktail of measures which are partly drug-based and partly lifestyle-based.

Will this work? It is still much too early to know how far the theologically derived principles can contribute to finding a cure for diseases such as cancer. It is a field in which Christian medical researchers should be encouraged to explore. At the very least, if the Creed is our guide, one suspects that much current medical research may be looking in the wrong place for the cures to the big intractable diseases of our times – with an enormous expenditure and effort in their research being wasted. Like the story of the chemist and the artist in the wild country, they may be failing to read the signs – with death as a result in both cases. Much medical research is trapped within component-level methodologies, when what is needed is a systemic and theologically derived approach to healing.

The contrast between the two approaches could not be more marked. First, conventional medical research focuses largely on the sub-cellular level, and indeed is delving into yet smaller entities as is apparent in the latest round of scientific research into the genome. By contrast, the theologically derived approach examines the body at the level where the full characteristics of a system appear – the liver in the case we have been examining. Second, conventional drug-related research invariably attempts to discover a specific new molecular chain or compound which has the power to inhibit, block or break the cause-and-effect chain within the human body in order to suppress the symptoms of the disease in question. In simple jargon, scientists are looking for a 'magic bullet' which can be fired at the cancer cells or the surrounding functions which give rise to them, kill off the offending parts and leave the rest of the system functioning normally – a classic component-level intervention. By contrast, the theological approach first seeks to stimulate the body's own healing functions at the systems-level. Third, the systems-level approach recognizes that only a combination of interventions – some drug-based and others lifestyle-based, can restore the full functioning of the body's own health. The conventional approach looks for single mechanisms to suppress the symptoms of the disease.

These examples of the nature of 'total systems' and how to heal them when they become deformed or deficient can be replicated many times. In fact, it occurred to me that the entire world – No! the entire created universe – is made up of an indefinite number of interlocking systems; from galaxies to atoms, and from archangels to ice, rocks and stones. Every system, whether it comprises the liver, or a sustainable energy supply system, or a 'whole task' in the world of work, is both part of a bigger system and, in turn, contains many sub-systems. These, again, contain smaller sub-systems, and so on throughout the height and breadth of creation. Some systems are inanimate and are governed by the laws of physics; others are social systems; others again cosmic systems.

Now here is an incredible thought! Each system, of whatever size or complexity, is composed of the dimensions of 'being' which are themselves manifestations of God as Holy Trinity. The Trinity must therefore pervade the whole of creation from top to bottom. Every created being must, in principle, be a reflection of the three divine persons.

We, as human beings, are seldom aware of this fundamental reality. We tend only to see creation in its outward manifestation, through our senses. I am sitting in my study and I see around me a chair, my diary, the carpet, the curtains and the sky outside. I do not readily perceive these as holistic systems, nor does my mind habitually recognize the divine strands by which they are held together as existent beings. However, the trinitarian structure of creation is as real as the specific objects we can see, feel and touch. When this is understood we begin to perceive creation from a quite different perspective, rather like those curious stereoscopic pictures which, if one looks hard enough, turn from being a jumble of meaningless lines and patterns to a three-dimensional picture of a flower or of floating clouds. Just so, I believe, we can learn to see all surrounding objects and beings primarily as manifestations of the Holy Trinity, rather than as mere physical entities to be used, abused or consumed. Such a reorientation of perspective is, I believe, an essential precondition for healing the sufferings of the planet.

CHAPTER 20

The Teambuilding Dispositions

If the trinitarian Creed is the basis for the regeneration of all physical, social and economic structures and systems, how does this relate to the ultimate goal of a spiritual renewal in Christ? What is the connection? How can a person be drawn from participation in 'whole' structures into a deeper spiritual life? We asserted earlier that within the world of work, holistic structures only gave the opportunity for increased motivation and personal development. How is this opportunity to be turned into an actuality?

I had a theory which I wanted to test. Where it first came from I no longer know, but it fitted nicely into the overall framework of theological and empirical ideas about work which had been developing so far. I called the theory 'the triple jump'. It postulated that if through work we could reach salvation, i.e. total unity with God and with each other, we could do so in three steps. First there was the hop from 'unstructured disorder' to 'structured groups' who could plan, do and evaluate 'whole' tasks; then the skip from 'structured groups' to 'cohesive teams'; and then the jump from 'cohesive teams' to 'divine unity'.

Step 1, from 'disorder' to 'structured groups', had already been achieved many times throughout my consultancy work. It was, moreover, possible to replicate such a positive transformation on a large scale, since the benefits both to the people themselves and to the efficient operation of the organization were plain to see.

Step 2 was more problematical. How does one turn a 'structured' group into a 'cohesive team'? A group of individuals with no obligations to one another into a mutually supportive fraternity?

About Step 3 I had no idea.

My interest in teamworking was awakened because, having structured work using the seven principles for many years, I gradually came to notice a recurring phenomenon. Every time the new structures were put in place, and when the benefits were visible, there came from the workgroups and management involved a spontaneous desire to develop teamworking among themselves. It was as if, having settled in the new improved structures, people were asking: 'Where do we now go from here?' There was clearly a demand; people were asking for help. We therefore formed a small think-tank to study ways of introducing teamworking. The year was 1991.

I was fortunate in having come to know a number of first-class practitioners in the field of organizational change, and teamworking training. As well as being experienced practitioners, what everyone had in common was a value system which if not explicitly Christian by name, was certainly so by nature. We met regularly for two years and from our deliberations there emerged what have come to be called the 'Six Teambuilding Dispositions'. These are six behavioural traits which if acquired and practised regularly will produce teamworking.

The dispositions are:

1. A resolve always to value one's own skills and those of others.

2. A willingness to listen and to communicate honestly and purposefully with one another.

3. A commitment to help and encourage one another.

4. A readiness to extend trust to one's leader, who earns this trust by striving to maximize the team's welfare and performance.

5. A feeling of responsibility for the team as a whole, as it works for the successful completion of a worthwhile task.

6. A willingness to contribute one's own creative inputs and to allow them to be transformed into other, better team outputs.

With hindsight, it is easy to rationalize how the dispositions were formed. We were devising a series of propositions which were halfway between the seven work structuring principles and the key demands of the Gospels. Of course, in reality it was not quite so straightforward. As with other incursions into a theology of work it was more a case of first having a rough idea of the solution and then gradually working on it until it assumed its final shape, rather in the same way as a fine piece of sculpture slowly emerges from the rough-hewn rock.

In addition to these dispositions, we also developed a training programme to help participants understand and practise the dispositions in a learning environment. The programme was designed to include 'best practice' methods and techniques drawn from the wide experience of the working team.

The close correspondences between the dispositions and the work structuring principles on the one hand, and between the dispositions and the precepts of the Christian Gospels on the other, gave us a further insight. Once again, there appeared to be a synergy between the practical experiences of expert behavioural scientists and managers and of the experience of Christian faith.

The first teambuilding disposition states that group members should learn to value their own skills and those of others. This ties in closely with the work structuring principle that each workgroup member should carry out a meaningful job, the principle based on the role of the church as 'body'. The principle says 'Design whole jobs which utilize the creative skills of the group members,' and building on this, the disposition says 'Value the skills and contribution of each member of the body, including your own.' Out of this mutual respect comes greater confidence, and from confidence springs a uniquely creative contribution from each team member, and from unique creativity is developed vocation. One's vocation in turn ultimately relates to the gifts of the Holy Spirit, as Paul said:

> Now to each one the manifestation of the Spirit is given for the common good. To one there is given through the Spirit the message of wisdom, to another the message of knowledge by means of the same Spirit, to another faith by the same Spirit, to another gifts of healing by that one Spirit, to another miraculous powers, to another prophecy, to another distinguishing between spirits, to another speaking in different kinds of tongues, and to still another the interpretation of tongues. All these are the work of one and the same Spirit, and he gives them to each one, just as he determines.
>
> *1 Corinthians 12:7–11 (NIV)*

It is no coincidence that the passage immediately following contains Paul's description of the church as body.

The second teambuilding disposition is similarly a halfway house between a work structuring principle and the earthly manifestation of the divine unity. The disposition is to be willing to listen, and to communicate honestly and purposefully with one another. This corresponds to the work structuring principle that each workgroup should be able fully to evaluate its performance against agreed standards of excellence. The principle ensures that the external conditions for full evaluation are present; the data, the communications channels, the feedback system. The disposition is necessary if these facilities are to be properly used. Without being prepared to listen and to communicate honestly and purposefully, there is little point in tossing data about. Yet both the principle and the disposition are themselves only precursors to the spiritual goal of being 'empty' of one's own ego so that one can perceive the needs of others, in the sense that Mary became 'nothing' in order better to accept her son Jesus' mission in the world.

The third disposition, being willing to help and encourage one another, is the inner psychological state needed to enable the small group to function cohesively. It is the 'bridge' between the outer structural principle (i.e. that the basic organizational unit should be the primary workgroup) and Christ's commandment to 'love one another as I have loved you'. On the one hand, without the existence of the group in the first place, it becomes physically difficult to help and encourage one another, since people do not have the advantages of proximity and familiarity. On the other hand, to help and encourage one another is a stepping-stone to the heroic demands of the gospel, where Jesus asks us to love to the point of being willing to die for one another.

Again the disposition to extend trust to one's leader, who earns his trust by striving to maximize the team's welfare and performance, is contingent upon the structural requirement that there is a leader in the first place. It also presages the Christian's unqualified commitment as expounded in scripture of total obedience to the church or monastic order to which he or she belongs. It is interesting, incidentally, that when a team practises this disposition, both the team and its leader come to recognize more and more clearly how important it is to have a leader, what the leader's unique value-adding role really is, and how helpful that role is to the successful functioning of the team and the development of its members. In fact it is no exaggeration to say that the deeper and stronger the degree of teamworking, the greater the need to obey a leader. Teamworking enables one to understand the connection between love and obedience.

Turning to the fifth disposition, the structural right of the workgroup to plan and organize its own work can only be translated into teamworking if group members willingly accept the responsibility for the outcomes of the group as a whole, and not just for their own individual contribution. We all know people who do their own job well, but who will always leave the premises promptly when their working time has elapsed, while others won't leave until they are sure that the group's task as a whole has been completed satisfactorily for the day. The fifth disposition is the precondition for the faithful stewardship by all Christians in relation to creation as a whole.

Finally, the sixth disposition requires that group members are willing to contribute their own creative inputs, and allow them to be transformed into other better team outputs. This is the psychological equivalent to the basic transformation in work processes, where the raw materials 'die', so a new product can be 'reborn'. It asks that inwardly, each person should be willing to risk giving up the 'raw material' of his or her own ideas in order that it can be subsumed or absorbed into the pool of other ideas being contributed by other team members, so that a new and better 'product' of the team's combined endeavours can be created. This process in turn echoes the real spiritual task of the Christian which is to 'die' to himself in order to participate in the resurrection experience of enjoying the new life in Christ. 'Take up your cross and follow me,' said Jesus.

In all these cases, not only are the dispositions essential if proper teamworking is to be established, but they are at the same time a tremendously helpful stepping-stone towards an authentic commitment to a Christian life of love and faith.

For many people, though not all, such an intermediate step is essential if the gap between selfish individuality and divine unity in Christ is to be bridged. It is a fact that only a few are making the leap to such faith in one jump, especially those deeply estranged from God from within a materialistic urban/industrial environment.

I have had several experiences which confirm the psychological and spiritual efficiency of the dispositions. Real fruits, spiritual and material, have come through practising them. For example in the early days of their development, in a pilot workshop, I and other members of the think-tank acted as guinea-pigs and took part in a teambuilding course, during which we all practised the dispositions in a learning environment. We used as the training model the course which we had previously designed. We also invited some 'outsiders' to take part, in order to test their reactions.

The results were highly encouraging. To start with, as we began to practise the dispositions there was a certain measure of self-consciousness and mild embarrassment. But after a couple of days, as our understanding of the dispositions deepened and we began to practise several at the same time, a bonfire of collaborative goodwill was lit. Creativity flourished; deeper personal relationships were made; the 'output' of the group increased dramatically; the supportive cohesion was noticed by outsiders; and everyone learned a lot about themselves from the experience. We were all delighted with the outcome.

There were many incidents which surprised and pleased us. We found, for example, that the unity of the group was as strong in non-working time as it was during the course itself, for example during the do-it-yourself preparation of breakfast, or during the washing-up. On many management courses the same minority of stalwarts do the chores while the rest with uncanny timing disappear until the work has been done! In our case everyone contributed fully, and we were all astounded at the speed and efficiency with which the work got done. We also found that everyone brought with them a unique contribution to the success of the course that was quite unrecognized at the outset. One person was especially good at defusing personal worries, another at ensuring a right balance between work and leisure, another at raising our morale through his infectious sense of humour, another by seriously and gently refocusing our minds on the deeper 'essentials' of what we were trying to do, another in supplying the conceptual framework of ideas which informed the project work, another in keeping our deliberations practical and properly earthed, another at carrying the responsibility for seeing that the work was completed thoroughly and on time and so on. What is more – and this was crucial – all these things were achievable within the natural human order. Though the conversation sometimes turned to spiritual topics, it did so quite naturally and easily; there was no proselytizing. We were simply rediscovering our natural birthright as human beings.

I already know that the participants on our private course, and indeed on other courses we have since run or sponsored, have felt moved to deepen their own inner lives as a result of their experiences. They are drawn closer to God because they have felt, often for the first time, the thrill of unity in a warm, effective and strongly bound cohesive team operating within divinely compatible structures. Within this supportive environment the experience has triggered off changes in their personal attitudes and relationships. Through the dispositions the divinely inspired healing process advances further.

CHAPTER 21

From 'Whole' Work to 'Whole' Businesses

Let us imagine a well-structured theologically compatible workplace environment. There is a small workgroup, whose members are carrying out all the planning, doing and evaluation activities necessary to accomplish a 'whole' task. They are working as a closely knit team, with meaningfully differentiated job roles under a leader whose role is to coordinate the group's activities, empower, coach and motivate the group members so that the group's task can be completed successfully. The technology and tools used by the group allow group members to use and develop their creative talents, and the working space is laid out so that the group can interact naturally and spontaneously. The Six Teambuilding Dispositions are being practised.

What I have just described is no different from a well-run stand-alone small business (or farm for that matter), consisting of up to about twenty people who, between them, do everything necessary to invent, make and sell a product or service. From a theological point of view they are re-enacting, in principle at least, the central features of the Christian faith: they are participating meaningfully in a creative act of transformation of nature, in a self-responsible, freely given, collaborative experience in which both the work and its rewards are fully shared. They re-enact, by analogy, the eucharistic sacrifice in which the small Christian communities broke bread together. Together they form a 'company' – *cum pane*, the Latin for 'with bread'.

The positive echoes of the spiritual order experienced at work don't end when the group member goes home. The resonances continue, and spill over. A happy fulfilled person at work is more likely to bring positive attitudes to his or her home than someone who brings back frustration and stress. If the dispositions are practised within the disciplined context of work, they tend also to become an acceptable norm in the home. More importantly, when work resonates with the divine, the natural goodness in every person is strengthened and his or her ethical sensitivities become sharper. Empirical evidence is accumulating that people doing meaningful work play a more active and constructive part in their local community than people doing meaningless work. Then discernment of right from wrong also becomes clearer.

But (I hear the reader saying to him or herself) all this may be desirable but isn't it somewhat impractical to advocate a wholesale return to small businesses? To which my reply is: 'Yes, I agree, it is impractical and I am not advocating it.' The point is that small businesses are not the only theologically compatible structural forms of work organization.

Imagine, say, four small businesses making the same product range, and operating out of the same business park. They are completely autonomous and stand-alone. Now let us imagine that the managing directors meet, say, for a drink in the local pub. The conversation turns to the difficulties each of them are experiencing in running a very small business, in other words, having enough time to both make and sell their products, the shortage of money to buy the best equipment and so on. At a certain point, let us imagine, one of the managing directors says: 'Why don't we combine our sales forces so that we stop doing everything four times, and gain some economies of scale?' Another managing director adds, 'And why don't we also share overheads like photocopiers, telephones, receptionists, etc.?' The third managing director chips in: 'We could also make much better use of our engineering people if they combined into a small group to service all of our equipment.'

So the four managing directors work out a plan, and combine their businesses. But they do it in such a way that the 'wholeness' of the work is undiminished. The four manufacturing workgroups are still intact. The difference is that other new groups have been formed in the combined businesses: a sales team, an administration team and an engineering team, for example. All these teams, it will be noted, still perform 'whole' tasks in their own disciplines. The work of the engineering group, for example, contains the basic transformation of 'breakdown' to 'working machine'.

In other words, 'whole' work can be built into larger-scale organizations if one takes care to preserve the smallness of its components – smallness within bigness. Then one can benefit from the economies of scale as well as keeping work 'whole'. But only up to a point. As organizations grow, they invariably reach a size where it becomes impossible to expand any further without destroying the 'wholeness' of work within its parts. Beyond this point not only do the theological resonances disappear, but it can be demonstrated empirically that net diseconomies set in, in both human and operational terms. Put plainly, when work ceases to be 'whole' the factory or office becomes more alienating and less efficient than when work is 'whole'.

It would be misleading to try to quantify in terms either of manning levels or financial turnover, when the maximum size of a factory or office is reached, and after which diseconomies set in. It depends partly on what the work processes are and on the variety of products or services provided. As a rough rule of thumb, however, once a factory or office as a whole exceeds approximately 200 to 300 people, problems are likely to occur.

Why does excessive scale produces negative effects on 'whole' work? The reason is that 'whole' work can only take place if a small workgroup plans, does and evaluates a 'whole' task, including a basic transformation. However, each work process only contains a given number of basic transformations. For instance, there is only one basic transformation in the process of turning iron into steel. This is a result of the laws of nature – it's God-given. If one can design a steelworks so that a small group of four to twenty people carries out the transformation (and the rest of the 'whole' task) then each worker, by virtue of the close collaboration and communication that naturally occurs within the same workgroup, can participate meaningfully in the 'whole' task. The task can also be planned and evaluated by the group with its leader, and the theological correspondences are thus complete. But if the scale is too big, this correspondence can no longer be maintained. In a very large steelworks sixty to a hundred people may be employed on the primary processes, and at the same time. This is true of many steelworks today. There is still only one basic transformation, but most people cannot participate in it. Also, because 'whole' tasks consist of an interrelated cluster of activities (like the life-cycle of Christ), parts of 'whole' tasks cannot be fully planned or evaluated, so most people are still further removed from their theologically derived exemplar. Yet the planning and evaluation still has to be done so other people and more layers of management have to be brought in, thus compounding complexity and inefficiency. Why, then, do people build larger units?

What often goes wrong is that decision-takers responsible for business strategy normally base their investment decisions on three main factors. The first is the projected demand for the product; the second is an implicit belief in the so-called technical economies of scale; and the third is accessibility to the market. Within a given accessibility, their belief is that 'bigger is better' regardless of the consequences.

What the decision-takers rarely do, on the other hand, is base their investment decisions on building 'whole' work around people or, as the encyclicals have expressed it, they do not start with the primacy of the human being. There are understandable reasons for this, notably that the decision regarding the scale of the facility is usually made by financiers and planners before work organization issues are considered. The 'whole' work designers therefore don't get a look in. The potential for 'whole' work is largely eliminated before a single brick has been laid or a single employee recruited.

Investment processes which ignore the imperatives of 'whole' work need to be vigorously challenged, since the reality is that large-scale organizations also attract major diseconomies. These include the lack of flexibility of very large investments when product or market conditions change; excessive transport costs, resulting from centralized production; relatively high wastage of raw materials, which have to be within very tight specifications for large-scale processing; poor motivation, higher absence rates and worse safety records among employees; more communications breakdowns; higher insurance risks; acute vulnerability to big financial losses if demand falls and high fixed costs have to go on being paid; a greater risk of total shut-down if faults occur; and a product less attuned to the diverse demands of different and discerning customers.

The truth is that there is an optimum scale where at the systems-level the advantages are the greatest and the disadvantages the least, and this size is completely compatible with 'whole' work. There is quite a lot of empirical evidence to support this. Many studies on the relationship between profitability and size of corporations have shown that facilities with more than 200–300 people within them are not more profitable than smaller establishments, and are often less so. Some studies go further and suggest that the highest profitability is attained precisely by the medium-sized firms employing the few hundred people we have been advocating. What is certainly clear from all the evidence is that there are no economic disadvantages to firms employing hundreds rather than thousands of people. It appears that the technical economies of scale already reach frontier levels at these levels of manning, while the social diseconomies of scale also get worse when firms grow much beyond medium size.

Apart from size, another fundamental set of decisions which can greatly diminish the 'wholeness' of work is the choice of technology. There are technologies which are compatible with 'whole' work, and technologies which are not. One factor is the amount of automation. Excessive automation can remove the worker from the creative aspects of work and leave him a bystander, alienated and de-skilled. A wrongly designed assembly line, as the example of the washing-machine factory quoted earlier showed, is another case of a technical design incompatible with 'whole' work. Many other technological deviations could also be cited. These too can be shown to be less efficient.

A third area where new plant design decisions can diminish the wholeness of work is layout. Lumping together the wrong machines, or putting work in the wrong place, can destroy 'whole' work just as effectively as excessive scale or technology.

There exists, in fact, a large number of ways in which wrong decisions can produce work which is not 'whole'. These are now well understood and it is relatively easy to identify the material reasons by which the deformations are brought about. But why these errors persist is another question. What induces human beings repeatedly to take decisions which they know are patently destructive, psychologically harmful, socially divisive and operationally inefficient? To answer we must look behind the material to the spiritual causes. We might start by asking what theology has to say about the processes by which things start to go wrong. Evil enters here.

CHAPTER 22

The Deformation of Work

For a time while I was working at British Steel in London, quite coincidentally my father was working at the National Coal Board next door. We used to lunch together every now and then in a favourite haunt of his down the road, a little basement restaurant called the Polognia. Not surprisingly it was Polish, but more surprising were the waitresses. Each of them had a number tattooed on her arm. They were all survivors of Auschwitz.

I suppose it was fitting therefore that our conversation turned one day to the subject of evil. 'What is evil?' I wanted to know. 'How can there be evil if God is good?' As we were walking back to our offices my father told me a little story which has ever since stuck in my mind. He had read it in one of Dorothy L. Sayers' books. I have never found the original story so I might have the details wrong, but here it is. 'Imagine Shakespeare inventing the character of Hamlet. Before he invented him there was "no Hamlet"; then there was "Hamlet". Hamlet has a personality, he has strengths and weaknesses. However, because Hamlet exists there arises a new possibility, namely the possibility of inventing another person with the personality and strengths and weaknesses that are different from Hamlet. Let us call him "non-Hamlet". Then a further possibility arises, in that "non-Hamlet", who has free will, may choose to become "anti-Hamlet". It may be that he is not endowed with Hamlet's outstanding qualities, and becomes jealous of Hamlet and hates him.' My father went on. 'In just the same way, when God created human beings he could not help but create the metaphysical possibility of other classes of being, some of whom (insofar as they too had free will) could choose to destroy human beings. Do you see?' said my father, 'The possibility of evil is part of the very act of creation itself. It must necessarily take place when some created being freely chooses it.'

I found this explanation extremely helpful at the time, as it allowed me to understand a little better the theological definition of evil as 'the absence of a good which should otherwise be there'. I took that to mean that evil in its essence is not something real: God didn't create it; he only allows it. What God created was 'very good'. Evil by contrast is a defilement, a deficiency, a perversion, an abnormality brought about deliberately through someone's free will. I had another thought. If there could exist someone who was anti-Hamlet, there could equally exist someone who was anti-human or even anti-Christ. With a chill I remembered the sickening feeling of evil on the hill above Lake Vyrnwy. This evil wasn't just an abstract metaphysical concept. It was horribly real. Evil may start out as a deficiency but it rapidly develops into the deliberate intention to subvert God's will, either through self-indulgence, violence or sheer malice. Then evil turns to actual pain.

I discovered the same evil in work. When God as trinity is fully present in human work, and when the workgroup emulates the church as the mystical body of Christ, work is 'whole' and is 'very good'. When the Trinity and the church are not fully present there is a deficiency, a lack of a good that should properly be there. When someone begins to exploit the deficiency for their own ends, then there is evil in the work.

If the originating power attributable to God the Father is lacking, and the workman feels powerless in his work, because someone else has seized control, there is evil. If the work lacks a full measure of the presence of the Son and the worker experiences fragmentation because someone has deliberately designed an alienating assembly line, there is evil. If the work lacks the creativity and good purpose which comes from the Holy Spirit, and the work is meaningless to the workman, there is evil.

Today, after over two centuries of industrialization, in many factories and offices there is little resemblance to 'whole work'. There is a lot of alienation, evil and suffering. Organizations are much larger than the 'ideal' size; work is not organized around the basic transformations in the process; the workforce do not share in the 'wholeness' of work – they are organized according to the principles of division of labour and functional specialization; the 'doers' are separated from the 'planners'; leadership is eroded; there is excessive job demarcation and lack of communication, and so on. There is, in short, a gulf between what actually goes on in the world of work and what should ideally prevail. The same is true of the health sector and most other parts of the economy. Let us explore in more detail the means through which work loses its wholeness and metaphysically becomes 'evil'.

First, there is the originating or planning aspect of work. This involves notions of span of control, power, freedom to create, ownership, etc. To the extent that the workman or workgroup cannot participate fully in these aspects of the work, it may be said that the work becomes deformed in relation to God the Father. Such deficiencies may be manifested either at the psychological or at the economic levels. At the psychological level, the deformation of work is experienced as powerlessness and this occurs where there is a loss of discretion or freedom to originate or plan the work. At the economic level, the deformation may be described by the generic phrase 'loss of ownership'.

There is a second group of deformations which belong to the 'do' phase of work and are deformations in relation to God the Son. These occur whenever the workgroup only carries out a portion of the span of operation which comprise a 'whole' task. Let us call this task fragmentation. Task fragmentation not only destroys the creative opportunities inherent in work, but also generates the problems of division of labour touched on earlier in this book.

The third class of deformations occur when there is no opportunity for the workman to self-evaluate and correct his performance or perfect the article he is making in terms of its beauty and usefulness to society. These are deformations in relation to God the Holy Spirit. These failings may be observed today in processes in which man has become an appendage to the machine, through de-skilling through excessive mechanization and automation and also when there is inadequate feedback and knowledge of results. Psychologically the work becomes meaningless to the workman.

It should also be said that although a deformation in work may primarily affect the planning, doing or evaluation phase of work, it actually embraces all three together. Loss of ownership, task fragmentation and de-skilling are inherent in each other. This is because, if theologically the three persons of the Trinity cannot be separated, nor can the effects of their absence. A workgroup carrying out a small part of the task, for example, clearly cannot own the 'whole task' in its full psychological or economic sense – nor can its members properly evaluate and perfect the finished product.

Historically, also, these negations are closely interdependent. For example, the loss of ownership of the means of production by the artisan to the capitalist in the eighteenth and nineteenth centuries gave the latter the labour force and financial opportunity to invest in highly mechanized enterprises based on task fragmentation. Again, excessive mechanization reduces job opportunities and so exacerbates loss of ownership. So a vicious circle develops with a deviation in any one aspect of the 'whole' task having repercussions on all other aspects.

Loss of ownership, task fragmentation and de-skilling, then, in their very essence, destroy the wholeness of man's work. These are three 'pivotal' or 'nodal' errors affecting the structure of modern industrial work, from which all other structural errors flow. All represent a 'taking away' from human work something which should rightly belong to it.

Turning now to the workgroup and ways in which wholeness in the social relationships within it can be destroyed, these fall into three broad areas, reflecting the definition of the church as the mystical body of Christ. This translates into diseases of differentiation within the workgroup, diseases with respect to group integration and diseases concerning its leadership. In the language of organization theory, it could be said that there may be deformation in relation to job design, group participation and authority.

Perhaps the most common deviations to be found with regard to job design are those where individual jobs are too narrowly circumscribed, and there is excessive division of labour as well as rigid demarcation between jobs. When these occur both inefficiencies and poor motivation result. A contrasting error is that of enforced job rotation in which workers are compelled to rotate through each other's jobs. These common industrial practices distort the true interdependent yet functionally distinct characteristics of members of a common body.

As regards deviations from group participation, a familiar experience in many workgroups is simply that there is none, either because of structural obstacles, such as those mentioned earlier, or because the teambuilding dispositions are not being practised.

Finally, there exists a whole series of deviations with respect to the use of authority in the workgroup. These range over a wide spectrum from those who deny that there should be a leader at all, to those who put him in the position of a tyrant or autocrat. In between these extremes lie many other shades of error. Neglect of the leader's teaching role is one of the more frequent, as is the failure to understand the leader's special relationship with the major process transformation.

It is hoped that this cursory analysis will have pointed to at least some of the theological causes of the deformation of work and will enable readers to relate them to their own experience of working life. Unfortunately the imprint of these deviations in work today is everywhere apparent. I am not referring to the proliferation of different kinds of work, which stems partly from mankind's increasing domination over nature, but to the quality and integrity of the work itself. There is no need to dwell on the meaninglessness and triviality of much work to be found in modern society today. Its laboriousness is only too evident, its creative content too often diminished. In the words of Pope Pius XI:

> And so bodily labour, which even after original sin was decreed by Providence for the good of man's body and soul, is in many instances changed into an instrument of perversion; for from the factory dead matter goes out improved, whereas men there are corrupted and degraded.
>
> *Pope Pius XI, 'Quadragesimo Anno'*[6]

The trouble is also that a deficient work practice is rarely isolated but, like a contagious disease, it invariably impacts on other adjacent aspects of work, and so sets in motion a spiral of corrosion. There is, unfortunately, a logic of corruption, by which one bad practice leads to another.

In the first place, the deformation of work at the workplace invariably leads to the deformation of the work system as a whole.

Consequently, it affects the way factories and offices are designed. If one could structure work so that it conformed completely to the seven theological principles, most factories and offices would look very different from those existing today. In other words, there is a connection between the structure of work within a factory or office and the physical shape of the factory or office itself.

I still needed to find out whether there was a connection between the shape of work, the shape and size of factories in general, and the physical structure of society as a whole. In other words, is it true that if work does not conform to its divine exemplar it eventually leads to many of the intractable problems society itself is currently experiencing? I suspected it was. Time and time again I had noticed, as in the parable of the wheat and the tares, that industrialization was not only producing positive wealth, but it was also having catastrophic side effects which were gradually undermining the environment, the quality of life, prosperity, and in the end industrial civilization itself.

CHAPTER 23

Rulers of the Darkness of This World

Today there is very little 'whole' work left in industrial society. Evil, in the sense of a 'falling short' in the world of work, is rampant. I don't of course mean that the workplace is infected with corrupt people. Most of humanity has to work, and all types and textures of humankind are to be found at work. And most of us are not responsible for how work is designed or organized.

On the other hand there are people whose job it is to design work. That is where the roots of evil in work appear. It is mainly the plant designers, engineers, architects, production managers, accountants and planners whose decisions result in deformed work. But in truth, they are not evil either. I have not yet met anyone who knowingly and deliberately designs work against what he or she believes to be in the best interests of their organization or profession. In any case decisions affecting work design are invariably collective rather than individual affairs. It is a technical-economic process in which several people take part. Where there are many people involved the process also becomes socio-political. Forces are therefore at work which transcend the individual. These express themselves as ideologies, cultures, politically acceptable or 'politically correct' attitudes and so on.

A typical example of a widely held ideology is the almost universally held belief by design engineers that more automation is 'better' than less automation. As far as I know this piece of ideology has never been proven! Yet it has profound importance for making work 'un-whole'. So how do these ideologies arise? What has caused the unquestioning acquiescence of so many intelligent people to industrial work patterns which clearly have no long-term future?

I once read a book which first awoke within me the thought that there was perhaps more to evil than could be explained by ignorance, inefficiency or neglect by specific individual people. The book was by an eminent and original French philosopher named Jacques Ellul. It was called *The Meaning of the City*. When I picked it up I did so in the belief that it would be about the historical development of the modern city, but I was mistaken. The book was concerned with the nature of the cities found in the Old and New Testaments, and especially with the growth and evolving role of Jerusalem up to its destruction. Mindful of the sacred power of the ark of the covenant, Ellul concluded that one could attribute spirits to cities. He suggested that cities can be possessed by conscious powers which give the city its ethos, its character and its culture – for good or ill. When anyone enters a city, says Ellul, they are immediately filled with the spirit of that city which moulds their behaviour, expectations and relationships with the city. When they leave, they walk out of the spirit and are no longer affected by it. Ellul (being French) cites Paris as an example. When anyone goes to Paris they are immediately infected by its gaiety, *élan* and unique atmosphere which appears to be completely independent of the people who live there or who migrate in or out.

I don't take Ellul's theories totally seriously, but they contain enough plausibility to make me wonder whether there might be similar phenomena present in the world of work. After all, no less a figure than Paul had said that:

> For our struggle is not against flesh and blood, but against the rulers, against the authorities, against the powers of this dark world and against the spiritual forces of evil in the heavenly realms.
>
> *Ephesians 6:12 (NIV)*

Were there 'principalities and powers' within the world of work, I wondered, who were accelerating the confusion and disorder I felt everywhere around me? Or could everything be adequately explained in terms of human mistakes, ignorance, ambition and other forms of human fallibility? Until 1985 I was quite comfortable in the thought that the deformation of work was primarily the result of a cumulative process of technical ambition and lack of vision. But then something happened to make me less sure.

I was working in some offices where nothing seemed to be going right. The office workers seemed listless and unhappy. Their managers were frenetically busy and their own bosses formed a small but highly powerful clique who ran the enterprise with a combination of obstinacy, neglect and bullying. The bosses of these bosses were the board of directors (who had hired me) and these were collectively weak. Although they knew of the sorry state of affairs in the business, they acquiesced in it.

Although I worked very hard to restructure the offices, I seemed to be blocked at every turn. Individually people were pleasant enough, but collectively they seemed to be locked into a system with which everyone was unhappy, but which defied any attempt to change it. Even outsiders, after working in the office for a short time, became infected with the same feeling of paralysis.

I seriously wondered about Jacques Ellul. Had I for the first time perhaps come across a 'spirit' which had settled in the office and was slowly destroying it? Eventually I began to look for signs. If there was a spirit, where was it located? How did it manifest itself? Were there any events or practices which suggested what nature it had? Gradually I began to discern some recurring features, fuzzy at first but becoming sharper with observation. The spirit, if that is what it was, felt evil; a sort of sullen deadness overlain with a brittle irrationality.

Eventually I sensed that its source seemed to be in the organization's information network. A series of interlocking computerized information systems had been installed over the years. The result was a situation where little or nothing could be done by anybody outside its pervasive influence. The trouble was that the computers were 'bewitching' people into making decisions which were often quite harmful and irrational.

I became more and more convinced that if indeed there were such things as spirits or dark powers, then here was one. But what should one do about it? How could it be got rid of? I knew absolutely nothing about exorcism, nor did I particularly want to. All I knew was that Christ had cast out demons by naming them. But could this be done in the modern day? And was there really something nasty out there, or was I imagining it? I became increasingly apprehensive.

Then one day it happened. With an imposing degree of certainty, the name of the spirit came into my mind. The name exactly matched the 'feeling' of evil and fitted the external environmental circumstances. It was the name of one of the older computer systems. I decided to share my suspicion with a few friends who were connected with the business. To my surprise they took it very seriously, and soon the word had spread around. The results were dramatic. All hell was let loose. Certain individuals closely associated with the 'named' computer system were almost apoplectic with rage. A vicious campaign of lies, innuendoes and slander was directed at me and soon afterwards the exercise was brought to a halt. I was thrown out.

Two years later I chanced to meet one of the managers from the same office. During the course of an unexpectedly friendly conversation I asked what had happened to the computer system. He smiled. 'Do you mean the "——"?', he said, naming the 'spirit'. 'Yes,' I said, alarmed. 'It went away shortly after you left,' came the matter-of-fact reply. 'How do you mean "it went away"?', said I, 'It was a comprehensive European-wide system.' 'Well, it's gone now,' said the fellow from the office. 'The computer system has been completely dismantled and good riddance too. It was a pain in the neck.'

CHAPTER 24

The Deformation of Industrial Society

How many of today's global crises are due to workings of 'the rulers of the darkness of this world' and how many to our own stubbornness and sinfulness I do not know. What is certain, however, is that the trinitarian structure of work has all but disappeared under the impact of huge forces over which no one seems to have control. And the consequence of this has been to unleash new pressures on society which have fundamentally damaged the inherent stability of earlier generations. Deformed work has led inexorably to a deformed society.

Historically, the first link in the cause-and-effect chain was the victory of the 'factory system' over the small-scale craft-based organizations at the beginning of the industrial revolution in the late eighteenth century. Before the industrial revolution work forms were still more or less structurally 'whole'. Small groups of people originated and transformed products of intrinsic worth to the community, both aesthetically and functionally. Work groups were of manageable size with clear leadership structures. Work and domestic life were intertwined and took place mainly in small towns, villages and rural areas within the secure web of the extended family.

As is well known, the industrial revolution changed all that. The new-found ability to harness huge amounts of energy (water power, steam and later oil and electricity), coupled with a revolution in machinery design, led to factories many times more efficient than the craft-based work forms before them. The price, however, was to destroy the 'wholeness' of work. The new factories were essentially alien in nature to pre-industrial craft-based methods which had sustained society during earlier centuries. The difference was that work was now being organized according to the principles of task fragmentation, a separation of owner from wage earner, and an all-pervading mechanization, bound together by the rigours of nineteenth-century discipline. These developments coincided with a massive falling-away from the church. These were the first steps in the progression from deformed work to a deformed society.

Once businessmen had realized that the new 'factory system' was much more efficient and profitable than the older small-scale, labour-intensive methods of the traditional craftsmen, there was nothing to stop the rapid spread of larger and more mechanized factories across the country. In contrast to the small workshops of the previous centuries, by 1816 the largest spinning mills in Great Britain were employing over 1,500 people, a number greatly exceeding the optimum from the human 'whole' task point of view. Similar developments were taking place in iron, non-ferrous metals, railway workshops, dockyards, ceramics, paper-making and some mining enterprises. We have already discussed how excessive scale invariably leads to the deformation of work.

One of the early consequences of the spread of large-scale modes of production was the concentration of industry. This was the next major structural change leading to the wider deformation of society. As output increased, so firms expanded and developed around them an infrastructure and other ancillary commercial facilities. These in turn attracted other like-minded entrepreneurs developing similar businesses. In the early years of the industrial revolution such concentrations often occurred near ready supplies of coal or mineral resources necessary for the new industries, or around the ports. Also new specialisms emerged and, with the concurrent improvements in transportation, new industrial products were forced upon areas hitherto insulated from the market. Local firms were put out of business and rural industries were destroyed. An inevitable consequence was the migration of labour from the once protected rural areas to the new industrial towns and mining areas, due both to the new opportunities for work provided by large-scale industrial production units and the rising numbers of people who had lost their trade or ownership rights in the smaller villages. These developments, in turn, contributed to the breakup of the extended family in rural areas and hastened the formation of an urban culture.

Urbanization and the growth of industrial towns and cities thus followed inevitably from the initial factory concentrations which in turn were caused by the deformation of work. This was certainly true in England during the early nineteenth century. As the historian Weber put it:

> it must be clear in every mind that the growth of these cities presents in England a typical instance of the effect which the growth of manufactures and development of the factory system, a system of centralized industry, has upon the distribution of the population.
>
> A.F. Weber, *The Growth of Cities in the Nineteenth Century*[7]

Those who migrated most to the cities tended to be the younger elements of the population. Away from family influence and rootless, the new urban immigrants also tended to marry young. The emerging industrial regions, therefore, showed higher marriage and fertility rates than the rural areas. Thus with the growth of urbanization came a new growth of population, the rise in numbers being related to the offer of new jobs. In eighteenth-century England, one-quarter of the population lived in towns; in 1850, one-half of the population; in 1900, three-quarters of the population. In the same period the population rose from 22.3 million to 38.2 million.

Urbanization and the growth of population in turn profoundly influenced the course of economic change, and generated a new wave of effects which stemmed from the deformation of work. Markets continued to expand, especially in the industrial counties which were growing much faster than the national average. Within the urban environment, also, old employment patterns, which had previously integrated human work and family life into a common framework, were inappropriate. The factories brought about a new discipline and the new industrial towns a new and fragmented urban culture.

As the towns expanded, work became geographically divorced from the family. In addition, as in the towns there were seldom gardens, smallholdings or payments in kind, the weekly wage packet became the only means of obtaining the necessities of life. In previous times, the informal barter economy was much larger, and money was not the only and monopolistic means of exchange. The early towns, too, lacked the elementary sanitation, health and housing facilities which had been less urgent in the rural setting and so generated a whole new set of material needs and new social problems of a gravity and scale hitherto unknown. Disease, open sewers, cramped squalid houses, crime and prostitution, child labour and the like all demanded a moral reaction, and this was expressed during the mid-nineteenth century as massive new forms of social control. Successive governments were compelled to introduce extended legislative programmes, especially in the areas of health, poverty, sanitation, education and conditions of employment in order to cope with problems which by and large had been self-regulating before the industrial revolution.

All these trends, themselves consequences of the deformation of work, generated the demand for a further series of goods and services. Since families were no longer as self-sufficient as their rural forebears, a new class of 'middle men' sprang up to fill the gap. The immediate and natural link with the land having been broken, new goods and services were needed to restore it artificially. The development of capital investments, such as roads, means of transport, sewers, lighting and a whole host of other facilities, and of services such as wholesalers and retailers, police and civil servants, was inevitable once the urban population had expanded beyond the point where it could largely support itself. Thus the expansion of large-scale industries was further stimulated. In the new industrial towns, also, a ready supply of labour and capital was available, the latter from the rapidly expanding banking and financial sector. Innovation was becoming cumulative, with one invention sparking off another. Raw materials were obtainable in abundant quantities from overseas, with the balance of payments being preserved by an even greater growth of exports of manufactured goods stimulated by a free trade policy.

The new large-scale factories themselves became even larger on account of the increasingly large and expensive plant and machinery which was being installed. Also, heavy machinery and capitally intensive plant increase 'fixed' costs (which are incurred whether goods are being produced or not); thus industrialists found themselves obliged to keep their plant running at the highest possible levels of capacity working. Prices were cut in order to expand markets further, which in turn led to pressures for new innovation to cut costs. Again, with increasing emphasis on cost reduction, innovation and expansion, factories increased further in scale, and so the self-reinforcing cycle quickened.

As the base of large-scale industry deepened, new features of the economy emerged which hitherto had hardly existed. Economically, perhaps the most important was the investment cycle. Before this stage cyclical variations in output had been largely linked to the state of the harvest in different regions. Now, as a consequence of the structural deformation of work, booms and slumps occurred which affected the whole of industry and agriculture. In the case of agriculture, the free trade policy and rising foreign competition made domestic farmers particularly vulnerable. Thus in the UK in the 1870s, for the first time, serious unemployment (as opposed to the pre-industrial state of under-employment) became a feature of the economy. This in turn encouraged the growth of organized labour in order to preserve minimum wages and conditions of employment. Consequently industrial unrest appeared for the first time as an endemic feature of the economic scene, and it was especially in the large-scale heavy industries, such as coal and steel, that the bitterest strikes and violence were to be found. In these industries the technology and the labour force were at their most massive and the men most alienated from the traditional skilled ways of working. Massive scale and technology were thus directly linked to the growth of trade-unionism and its subsequent gradual involvement in the political arena.

Meanwhile, on the employers' side, similar power groupings were developing. By 1870, falling prices, more severe competition and fears of labour militancy had led to a growth of employers' associations, cartels, and later to the outright amalgamation of separate companies into 'combines' or 'multiples' through vertical or horizontal integration. At this time, too, most of the rapidly expanding industries with large plant technology took advantage of incorporation, limited liability and raising capital from the public. From the human point of view again, all these developments led directly to a further loss of ownership rights to a relatively small number of shareholders who themselves had little direct industrial experience or contact with productive work.

As industrial output increased further, a number of new consequences of the deformation of work emerged. First, the national resource position deteriorated. From a position of relative self-sufficiency, in which trade had largely consisted of non-essentials, the country became critically dependent upon imports and exports for its very economic survival. While in 1688, the UK imported about 5 per cent of its needs, by the 1900s the proportion had risen to over 25 per cent. By 1918, about seven-eighths of all raw materials (except coal) and one-half of food supplies were imported.

Industry also became more differentiated. An independent engineering industry was established (which in turn did much to spread industrialization abroad) and the 'tertiary' sector began to develop in the form of industries such as entertainment, tourism and the like. Some of these 'tertiary' industries, like transport, banking, insurance, trade, finance, were themselves largely responses to the process of industrialization itself. Moreover, these industries gave rise to a whole new range of clerical and other white collar jobs, hitherto unknown, and (from the human point of view) mostly bereft of a job content which allows any real scope for purposeful self-development.

Another feature of the late nineteenth and early twentieth centuries was the development of entirely new forms of industry engaged in the manufacture of artificial chemical and related synthetic products, such as plastics and fibres. Powerful stimuli towards the development of these products were the shorter processing times needed for their manufacture as well as the growing scarcity of renewable raw materials. Costs were consequently reduced and output and profitability increased. All these developments again made a big impact on material standards of living, but this time at the expense of the environment.

At the same time, industry was becoming more rationalized. Up to the twentieth century, the growth of large-scale mechanization had proceeded sporadically in pace with the discovery of new forms of motive power and technological appliances. In the early 1900s came the systematic introduction of work measurement, methods study, time-and-motion and other forms of 'scientific management'. With increasingly heavy competition coming from abroad, from countries which themselves had begun to industrialize, many of the old systems of working were becoming uneconomic. Older, and often more humane, practices were abolished in favour of new 'rational' methods of working.

By the 1920s the interplay of these various factors was

beginning to cause a highly unstable economic situation. There was an uncontrolled incidence of booms and slumps with resulting unemployment and industrial violence. This was also a period of political ineptitude and crisis culminating in the Great Depression of the 1930s, and it followed inevitably from the combination of factors which themselves were the unavoidable fruits of large-scale production and the deformation of work. The Great Depression, in its turn, gave rise to a new feature in economic life, namely widespread government intervention in monetary and fiscal affairs. Keynesian policies were introduced to restore and maintain full employment and to level out the effects of the investment cycle. These included large amounts of capital which were introduced for industry to rationalize and re-equip on an even larger scale than before. After World War II, and particularly through the 1950s and 1960s, the need was felt to increase controls still further, and the concept of national planning gained respectability as a panacea for global stability. Five-year national plans were inaugurated which set growth and investment targets for all major sectors of the economy. Nationalization was another device designed to regulate the fluctuations (and profits) of key sectors of the economy after World War II.

On the social front, parallel developments were taking place. The severe consequences of the Depression served to reinforce the need for additional social services to those which had already emerged during the nineteenth century. The stage was thus set for the emergence of the welfare state and the modern role of government as a social and economic regulator. In more recent years such intervention has been made the more necessary because unrestrained urbanization has developed as a consequence of industrialization, and socially deprived ghettos have begun to appear in the big cities. These in turn have augmented urban decay and unrest through rising crime rates, deviancy and the breakup of the nuclear family, as witnessed in rising divorce rates and the growth of one-parent families. There has in consequence been a massive increase in government spending on the social services, housing, education and health, with a corresponding increase in the national debt and in the burden of taxation. Migration, meanwhile, and the concentration of industry, was reaching the point where not just the viability of village industry but regional prosperity was being jeopardized in the rural counties. To counter this, yet more government measures were introduced, this time to promote regional development and to encourage the mobility of labour. This has succeeded, in part, in ameliorating the regional population imbalance, but socially it has led to renewed mobility and economically to further distortions in the market.

CHAPTER 25

Deformed Work and the Contemporary Crisis

The huge forces unleashed by the deformation of work at the beginning of the industrial revolution have created a society which, as we celebrate the millennium, is on the verge of collapse. Prompted on the one side by the widespread availability of goods from industry and on the other by a growing alienation from both factory and town, the consuming public has become addicted to further increases in output and greater material prosperity, regardless of the consequences. Consumerism and the cult of economic growth have become today's ideologies.

Industry's response has been to broaden the range of its products still further (for example, synthetic foods and leisure goods), commit itself to heavier research and development (for example nuclear, aerospace and biological), rationalize, expand and automate. To maintain profitability, cost-cutting has been the driver leading to large-scale redundancies and unemployment, and higher stress for those left in work. The theological value of 'whole' work has disappeared almost without trace.

The destructive effects of deformed work have spread rapidly across the world since international trade, too, has become correspondingly more important. Industry has come to be increasingly dependent upon imported energy and raw materials, and the urban populations increasingly dependent upon imported foodstuffs. To offset this, renewed government emphasis has been placed on exports, which have become crucial for the survival of all the industrialized nations. As a result, the developed countries have exerted enormous economic pressures on the poorer Third-World countries, whose terms of trade have become so disadvantageous that huge foreign currency debts have accumulated. The danger of default is now critical in some instances and this could have disastrous repercussions on the international financial system. Third-World countries are also likely to exert growing cost pressures on the wealthy countries as world shortages increase of certain raw materials (notably oil, itself a consequence of large-scale industrial expansion). In the next phase of economic disintegration, therefore, the terms of trade will turn against the industrialized countries. In any event, with increasingly unstable international monetary conditions, many countries are already beginning to face major balance of payments difficulties. A deteriorating balance of payments is, however, but one aspect of the impending international financial crisis facing the industrial world at the present time. Borrowing rates are at unacceptably high levels and many Third-World countries are in chronic debt, reflecting the manifold symptoms of economic stress which have now emerged, not only in the industrial economies but worldwide.

One of the most intractable modern symptoms of the deformation of work is inflation. Economists disagree as to its main causes. Some say that it is due to excessive union demands for higher wages; others blame it on the scale of government expenditure; others point to rising raw material costs and the adverse swing in the terms of trade; others again think that there is too much available liquidity; or say it is the fault of a greedy and irresponsible public who will stop at nothing to increase their consumption. Whatever the exact reason, however, the fundamental causes of inflation are quite clear. The precondition for inflation was laid when people became solely dependent upon the pay packet for the necessities of life, as a result of urbanization. The pressures on costs have come with the response of the trade unions to the social effects of the business cycle and rising raw material and energy prices due to world shortages. Excesses in demand have come from an alienated and consumption-orientated urban public for whom work is meaningless and happiness means wealth. And all these features – the growth of urbanization, the emergence of the business cycle, the worldwide exploitation of raw materials, alienation and consumerism – are themselves products of the structural deformation of work. Industrial inflation, in other words, is an intrinsic concomitant of the deformation of work itself.

I have attempted briefly to trace the historical evolution of deformed work and its effects on society as the different forces it has unleashed have reacted on one another. The interactions are complex, and difficult to disentangle individually since many influences are at work simultaneously. However, underneath the historical complexity, certain inexorable cause-and-effect chains stemming from the deformation of work are clearly visible. They are listed below. Each chain also suggests a next stage which might reasonably be expected to come about if the causes of the deformation of work are left unattended. Some of the more obvious chains are as follows:

1. Deformation of work ☞ large scale units ☞ large scale firms ☞ combination of firms ☞ national ownership ☞ international ownership ☞ world control and government?

2. Deformation of work ☞ concentration of industry ☞ industrial towns ☞ unchecked urbanization ☞ social problems in cities ☞ ghettos ☞ rising crime etc. ☞ breakdown of city life?

3. Deformation of work ☞ destruction of village industry ☞ migration ☞ neglect of villages ☞ regional imbalances ☞ breakdown of rural life?

4. Deformation of work ☞ breakup of extended family ☞ nuclear family ☞ breakup of nuclear family ☞ single-parent family ☞ severe and continuous stress ☞ loss of personal identity?

5. Deformation of work ☞ large-scale units ☞ larger-scale machinery ☞ growth of capital goods industries ☞ investment cycle ☞ depressions ☞ cyclical unemployment ☞ structural unemployment?

6. Deformation of work ☞ division between owner and worker ☞ growth of organized labour ☞ industrial strife ☞ national confrontation between social classes ☞ 'two' nations ☞ political deadlock ☞ civil instability?

7. Deformation of work ☞ technical innovation purely for profit ☞ cumulative technological innovation ☞ pressures for cost-reduction ☞ development of cheaper synthetic materials and foods ☞ more research, including nuclear and biogenetic ☞ environmental pollution and sickness?

8. Deformation of work ☞ excessive output ☞ large-scale consumption of raw materials ☞ rising imports ☞ end of self-sufficiency ☞ dependence on overseas supplies ☞ vulnerability ☞ adverse terms of trade ☞ balance of payments crises?

9. Deformation of work ☞ widespread fragmentation of work ☞ alienation ☞ instrumental view of work ☞ more consumption ☞ more output ☞ consumerism ☞ cult of economic growth ☞ pressure on resources ☞ resource crises?

10. Deformation of work ☞ the factory system ☞ urbanization ☞ social problems ☞ government intervention in economic affairs ☞ changed role of state ☞ the welfare state ☞ massive government expenditure ☞ high taxes ☞ intrusion of government into other areas of life?

This brief review suggests that since the beginning of the industrial revolution, when work became structurally deformed, society has been evolving in a direction which is unsustainable. Whether on the political, economic, social, psychological, industrial or cultural front, there is occurring an inexorable logic which is leading to breakdown and collapse. Modern society which, uniquely, has been built up upon the foundations of new work forms is being ravaged by fatal deformations within the structure of this work itself. Deformed work, the leading edge of industrial society, is infecting society itself, just as a diseased organ in the human body eventually destroys life itself if unchecked. This is why a true theology of work translated into sound practical principles is of vital importance today. It is our task, together with all men and women of goodwill, to begin the process of reconstructing modern industrial work to avoid an otherwise inevitable collapse.

Epilogue

How can we begin to undertake such a fundamental task of reconstruction? This book would not be complete without sharing with the reader my own hopes.

First, although the downward spiral of corrosion has been evolving inexorably at least since the beginning of the industrial revolution, I am convinced that the time has never been more right for a rapid and comprehensive healing process to begin. Perhaps for the first time we are able to discern the real nature of the industrial crisis, its real spiritual roots and its destructive structural outworkings. The tide of change is also in our favour. The speed with which we can understand, communicate, respond to and implement change is far greater today than it has been for the past two centuries. My hope, therefore, is that the positive process of healing will greatly accelerate.

My second hope is that there may come forward, without delay, men and women of conviction and deep experience of the world of work who feel called to join the crusade to restore 'whole' work. Now is the time for action! Not only are the problems confronting us becoming greater with every day that passes, but so are the positive opportunities we will miss if we do not act now.

Third, I believe that anyone, however modest his or her station in life, can play a vital part in the healing process. God is not asking us to wait for government or the captains of industry to take the lead. He uses all of us, in our various

.ttle ways, to bring about his kingdom. All of us, by following the theologically sound, biblically based precepts of our faith, can influence the way we work to some degree, directly or indirectly. Each of us can light our own little bonfire of positive improvement. When lots of little fires are lit, they will fuse into a giant conflagration.

Finally, my prayer is that God may call you, the reader, to play your part. May he guide you, inspire you and commit you to this endeavour; and may you be joined by many others to carry out this immense task. May you be equipped with patience and with courage, and be given fuller and deeper insights into how to restore 'whole work' by using as your compass a true understanding of the trinitarian structure of God's creation, of the immeasurable wisdom of the Creed and of the mysteries of Christ's holy Church.

References

1. Chiara Lubich, *Jesus in the Midst*, New City Press, p. 37.

2. Chiara Lubich, *Jesus in the Midst*, New City Press, pp. 31–3.

3. Etienne Gilson, *The Christian Philosophy of St Thomas Aquinas*, Victor Gollancz, 1961, p. 195.

4. St Bonaventura, *De Reductione Artium ad Theologiam*, Opuscula II, St Anthony Guild Press, 1966, para 12.

5. C.S. Lewis, *Miracles*, Fontana, London, 1960, p. 116.

6. Pope Pius XI, 'Quadragesimo Anno', Catholic Truth Society, 1963, para 135, p. 53.

7. A.F. Weber, *The Growth of Cities in the Nineteenth Century: A Study in Statistics*, 1899, p. 43ff.

"Lorenza Collins"

=> Liberal arts
      ↑
   African diasporal study

=> Dub Poetry ⇐

" ldcollins11@hotmail.com "

=>